Discussion
Booklet III

**TO LIVE
IS
CHRIST**

TO LIVE IS CHRIST • Discussion Booklet III •
The Developing Human Community

Fully aware of religious education as a key factor affecting human relations, the editors invited a Protestant and a Jewish scholar to review material presented in this book as it bears on their respective faith communities.
These are Dr. Edward Zerin, Rabbi, who consulted with the American
Jewish Committee and Dr. Martin E. Marty, Associate Editor, *Christian
Century*. While their personal views and religious beliefs obviously must
differ from some of the views presented here, both feel that the content has
been so handled as to increase intergroup understanding. While it is hoped
that these distinguished authorities similarly will review forthcoming volumes in this series, new materials in preparation will have to await such
response at a future date.

the developing human community

William J. Kalt *and* Ronald J. Wilkins

HENRY REGNERY COMPANY  Chicago

Published with ecclesiastical permission.

Archdiocese of Chicago

September 23, 1967

The authors assume full responsibility for the final form and content of the text.

Passages from Sacred Scripture contained in the text have been rendered into English accommodated to adolescent comprehension by Father Brendan McGrath, OSB, and the authors.

CONTENTS

THE CITY OF MAN

ORLANDO CABANBAN

The dream

Beyond civilization

Civilization is entering a new phase.

We are no longer simply civilized men; we are living in the dawn of a new and more advanced age for which all the previous centuries of civilization have been laying the groundwork. Let us call the coming age *trans-civilization*.

It is not easy to draw a sharp dividing line between one age and another, for civilization is only beginning to end and trans-civilization is only beginning to begin. Only centuries from now, when trans-civilized men look back upon our times, will the difference between the two eras seem obvious. From their height of advancement a thousand years from now, trans-civilized men will regard us as primitive, much as we today regard pre-civilized and prehistoric cave man as primitive.

"Where is this trans-civilization you dream of?", a skeptic might ask.

Almost the same question might have been asked hundreds of thousands of years ago. "Where is this civilization you dream of?", skeptical cave men might have asked the inventor of the wheel. Would even he, genius though he was, have been able to foresee the pulley-wheels that would one day be used in Egypt to raise huge blocks of stone into gigantic temples and immense pyramids? Would he have been able to prophesy the application of teeth to wheels for the creation of gears and all the machines

3

they make possible? Could he have known about the paddlewheels that would one day move steamboats and generate electricity? Probably not. And yet we may surmise he did not doubt that with his rudimentary wheel a new stage of human living had been ushered into history.

But if pre-civilized man could point to the wheel as a symbol of the civilization yet to come, to what can we civilized men point to symbolize the trans-civilization yet to come? Isn't one new invention like another? Why should any particular invention or set of inventions be anything more than an expression of civilization as we know it? Why is it necessary to speak of a "new stage of history," a phase of human living which is as far advanced beyond civilization as civilization is advanced beyond prehistoric cave-living? For the answer, let us look at the symbol which represents trans-civilization.

Trans-civilization became possible when a man named Albert Einstein in 1903 wrote down on paper a revolutionary statement: $E = mc^2$. This simple sentence, the capsule formula for atomic power, is propelling trans-civilization into history just as really and symbolically as the wheel started civilization rolling.

The wheel, of course, was not the only civilizing instrument. There were others: the controlled use of fire, the invention of boats, the use of metal instead of wood, the internal combustion engine, etc. The wheel was probably not even the first of mankind's discoveries, but it is a symbolic one—for it is a clear indication of the creative power of man's mind. Fire could be found by anyone with eyes; but the wheel was not found with the eyes, it was patterned by a creative mind.

Similarly, atomic power is not the only trans-civilizing instrument; perhaps electricity is another, and certainly the electronic computer is one. But atomic energy is perhaps the most fitting symbol of man's ability to trans-civilize himself, for it is a clear indication of the creative power of man's mind. A spark of electricity can be generated by accident, but the spark of genius that generated the formula $E = mc^2$ was no accident; it was patterned by a creative mind.

Let us contrast these two symbols (the wheel, and atomic power) to see what they tell us about the two ages they symbolize.

The wheel made civilization possible by **extending** *man's powers.* The energy of one man can be made into the equivalent of the energy of many men. On wheels, one man can push a load it would take five or ten men to carry; by the use of pulley-wheels a particular lifting job can be reduced from fifteen man-hours to three; in an automobile a man can travel twenty times as fast as a man can walk. The wheel symbolizes man's ability to multiply his power.

But atomic energy symbolizes man's ability to **explode** *his powers*—to multiply them almost to infinity, as it were. The energy released for man's disposal can no longer be calculated on the human scale. Scientists are already talking seriously about the possibility of stopping a hurricane by setting off a hydrogen bomb in its eye. It is meaningless to try to calculate such a job in terms of man-hours; it is not a question of one man doing what would otherwise require many men, but of man doing what all the men in the world together could not do by any ordinary mechanical extension of their powers.

It is true that man's ability to explode his powers can be used for destruction as well as for creation. Through push-button warfare man can reduce the world to *non-civilization*. The dream of trans-civilization is a *prophetic one*—that is, it is a call to *make* it come true. It will not come true by itself. Men must *decide* whether to create or destroy.

Economics, politics, and culture

To understand the challenges which will face us in tomorrow's world, we need to understand the features of today's world which are preparing for it. Civilization as we know it has laid the groundwork for trans-civilization as your children and grandchildren will know it. Tomorrow's dream can only be built upon today's reality. Civilization has been a monumental achievement of man; over the course of thousands of years, it has changed man from a herd to a community. Only by appreciating and updating what civilization has made possible, will man be able to reach a new level of humanness in trans-civilization. For civilization has not only given us inventions, it has given us ways of dealing with our fellow man and traditions for understanding what is valuable in life. Trans-civilization based on new inventions will

5

make mankind more human only if man develops an ever keener sensitivity to his fellow man, an ever higher sense of values. If he does not, he will use his inventions to destroy himself.

What is man to do with the powers that are becoming his —these new tools to exploit the resources of the earth as never before? The answer cannot be found in the tools themselves. They must come from man. We must create a way of life in which these tools are our servants, not our masters. Scientific progress must be matched by a progress in our ways of dealing with our fellow man, and in our understanding of what life is all about.

In civilizing himself, man has built a social life which unites three areas of life: **economics, politics,** *and* **culture.** We must learn how these are related to each other if we are to understand how our world got to be the way it is and how it will get to where it is going. To live a full life in human society means being aware of how all three aspects of life are affecting us. Let us be clear about what we mean when we use these words.

Society as a whole is built upon the twin base of man's *economic* and *political* living arrangements. His *cultural* expression of life rests upon this base and gives meaning to it.

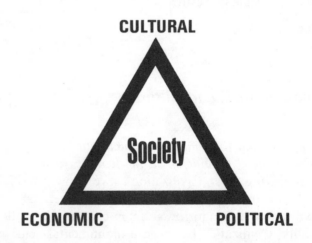

Let us examine each of these three aspects of life in detail.

1. **The economic base of civilization.** From the dawn of history, man has always been in need of food, shelter, and clothing. He has been dependent upon the *resources* available to him, has developed *tools* to exploit these resources, and has devised methods of *distributing* them.

6

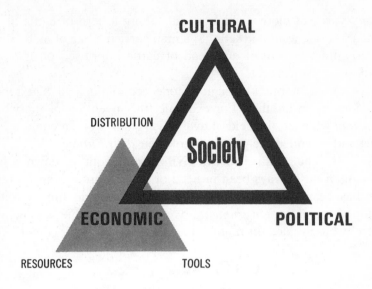

CULTURAL

DISTRIBUTION

Society

ECONOMIC   POLITICAL

RESOURCES   TOOLS

This **economic** or "Where's it going to come from?" side of life concerns all the human activities connected with *procuring the material roots* of life. It includes not only money, but such things as food, housing, health, and employment as a money-gaining activity. The economic life of society is built upon the twin base of available *resources* (food, farmland, timber forests, etc.) and the appropriate *tools* (pots and pans, tractors, sawmills, etc.) for processing the resources. With these as a foundation, man devises a system of *distribution* (transportation, money, market, etc.) of necessities to consumers.

Economic progress has come about whenever man created a major breakthrough in one of these categories. For example, land was always present to primitive man, but as long as he lived primarily from hunting and fishing he did not appreciate its full value as a *resource* (for he moved to new land when the animals he hunted moved); but when man learned to clear it for farming and to plant it regularly, particular areas of land became vastly more productive resources in his economy. Again, fire was known to man ever since the first bolt of lightning started the first known forest fire; but it did not become a *tool* until man learned to start it on his own, to cook food with it, to forge metal plows with it and so on. A third area of economic progress was that of *distribution:* metal took on a new usefulness when men learned to use it in the form of coins; instead of bartering so many cattle for so many yards of cloth (which meant taking a herd of cattle along whenever one went marketing), a man carried a bag of metal discs each with a picture of one head of cattle impressed on it*, and trade became easier.

Often, a breakthrough in one economic area had repercussions upon another. For example, the invention of the wheel as a *tool* widened the field of available *resources* man could transport and extended the possibility of their *distribution*.

2) **The political base of civilization.** From the dawn of history, man has always been in need of justice, order, and welfare. He has been dependent upon the *people* around him, has developed forms of *government* to regulate their interaction, and thereby has molded the many into a common-unity, or *community*.

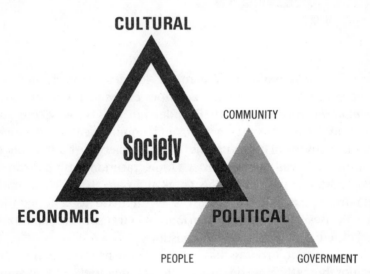

This **political** or "Who's responsible for doing what?" side of life concerns all the human activities connected with *structuring life into organizational branches*. It includes not only the government of nations and cities, but also such things as the division of responsibilities within a family. The political life of society is built upon the twin base of a natural grouping of *people* (a family, a school, a nation, etc.) and the appropriate system of *government* for organizing their interaction (family tasks, school rules and administration, national constitution and government, etc.). With

* From the Latin word *pecus* for cattle, which became applied to such coins, we get the adjective "pecuniary" which remains in use today as referring to monetary matters.

these as a foundation, man creates a *community* or orderly union of many people as one unit).

Political progress has come about whenever man created a major breakthrough in one of these categories. For example, when primitive men of one family or clan learned that man of another family or clan were not necessarily rivals or enemies, it was possible for them to enlarge their definition of what group they belonged to; they counted their own family or clan along with members of the other family or clan as all belonging to the same tribe; they were now one *people* and were able to trade, learn, and live on a wider basis. As such groupings of people became larger, their interaction became more complex and new systems of *government* were needed. One of the major breakthroughs was that of dividing and delegating authority (for example, reserving major decisions to a king but allowing minor decisions to be made by governors.) *Common unity* was significantly advanced each time a breakthrough in political barriers was achieved. For example, as men gradually learned to make their societies self-supporting by using the resources of nature without needing to use other *men* as resources (slavery, in other words) this economic progress made it possible to do away with political class distinctions which unnecessarily divide man from man. In general, the progress of common unity has come about through a growing sense of self-government by all the people rather than of some people being governed by others without their consent or representation.

3) **The cultural expression of civilization.** From the dawn of history, man has always been in need of a sense of meaning in his life. He has been dependent upon his fellow men for an *education* that brings him up to date with them in the quest for knowledge and the skills of survival; he has developed a *life-style* for holding together the many routines for living daily life; and he celebrates with his fellow men their common *vision of what life is all about*.

This **cultural** or "What's it all about?" side of life concerns all the human activities connected with *expressing the spiritual flowering of life*. As used in this sense, it includes art, philosophy, scientific theory, religion, love, personal life-style, etc. The cultural life of society is built upon the twin base of *education* (the three r's as well as whatever other basic skills and insights the community wishes to pass on to its new members) and the particular *life-style* (rural or urban, Western or Oriental, "Old

9

World" or "mod," etc.) which express this heritage in action. With these as a foundation, man gives expression to a *vision of life* which makes his life worth living.*

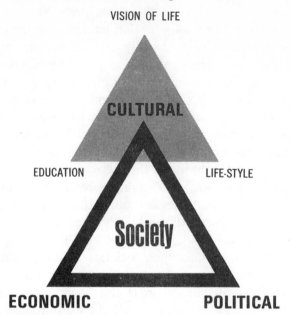

Cultural progress has come about whenever man experienced a major breakthrough in one of these categories. For example, the invention of the alphabet pushed *education* forward by making it possible to store accumulated information outside of mortal memories. Again, the development of the impersonal *style* of dealing with the many strangers one meets during a regular day in any large downtown area makes it possible for large numbers of people to get a lot done in close quarters without wasting one another's time. And in the area of *vision of life,* Christians believe that the growth of monotheism (belief in One God rather than many gods) has been a great advance in making life's meaning coherent.

The three areas of life (economic, political, and cultural) are closely related to each other. Development in one area brings about development in another. Through the complex interplay of development in all three areas, the human race has civilized

---

* Anthropologists and sociologists often use the word "culture" in a larger sense which includes the economic and political structures of a society as well. Here we are using a narrower definition of the word according to an accepted popular usage.

itself. Man has built a highly complex *economic* system to support him and a *political* structure to channel him in the *cultivation* of humanness.

A clear understanding of these three areas of social life is important for your understanding of our developing human community. Here is a random list for you to check how well you have understood the preceding section.

Before each item, write an E or P or C to indicate whether it is primarily an economic, political, or cultural item.

(Note: in some cases, an item might belong to more than one area. For example, a printing press is a *cultural* object insofar as it makes possible the spread of learning, and it is also an *economic* object insofar as it enables publishing to be a big business.)

__alphabet	__police station	__guitar
__Supreme Court	__credit card	__school regula-
__wheel	__Rembrandt painting	tions
__radio	__coal mine	__mink farm
__Baptism	__Thanksgiving Day	__stock market
__penicillin	__Charlie Brown	__Emancipation
__printing press	__paper money	Proclamation

In the remainder of this booklet we are going to focus on the **economic base of life.** We will not ignore politics and culture, but we will be viewing them through an economic lens—we will discuss political and cultural problems only insofar as they have economic causes. (Other booklets in the series will discuss the political and cultural aspects of life more thoroughly).

Crossing the Great Divide

Although civilization has not yet reached the same level of development in all parts of the world, still in the developed countries it has reached the point where we can begin to see the seeds of an entirely new phase of human living—the age of trans-civilization.

In our time we are living through what will come to be looked upon as the **Great Divide** of human history: the human community will be so vastly different after our time than it was before our time, that all the centuries since man first appeared on the planet one million years ago until now will be lumped together as the "preparatory phase" of human community, and the late 20th and early 21st century will be looked upon as the first days of the human community's really "coming into its own."

Those are big claims. Let us briefly look at some statistics in the *economic* order which have led many people to make these claims, and then make some projections in the *political* and *cultural* orders which these economic statistics imply.

Mankind's economic advances in civilization have drastically affected the balance of nature. Whereas formerly the human race had to struggle to keep its numbers up, today the advances of medicine and food production have limited infant mortality and lengthened life expectancy to such an extent that the world's population is *doubling* every 35 years.

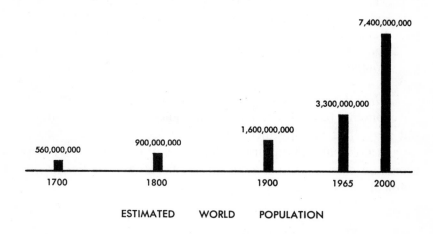

ESTIMATED WORLD POPULATION

Experts have computed that one-fourth of all the human beings who ever lived since the dawn of time are now alive! Your children or grandchildren will see the day when this proportion is increased to one-half and more. This means that during their life time it will be possible to say that, as far as numbers go, all the centuries since the first men until now constitute only the first *half* of human history; the *second half* of history is now alive all at once!

While the Great Divide in population is still being approached, it has *already been crossed* in energy consumption. Dr. Homi Bhaba, an Indian atomic scientist, computed a few years ago that, thanks to the continually growing number of factories, jet planes, rockets, and other fuel-consuming products of civilization, the human race has used as much energy in the past 100 years as all previous human beings had used in the previous 1900 years.* As our use of energy keeps doubling, especially due to the increased commercial use of atomic energy, trans-civilized man's consumption of energy will so greatly outweigh the energy-consumption of primitive men (who used only their own bodies, aided by animals, and small-scale uses of fire) that the *first half* of man's energy consumption throughout history will have lasted from roughly 1,000,000 B.C. until the 20th century; and the *second half* of energy consumption will be reckoned as beginning in the late 20th or early 21st century.

Again, statistics on the mining of metals from the earth tell a similar story. The year 1910 A.D. is roughly the year of the Great Divide for the extraction of many industrial metals and other raw materials.*

The age we are entering on the other side of all these Divides is aptly symbolized by the word "explosion." The curve of change in almost all areas is changing from a gentle straight-line slope to a steeply rising upward curve. The chart on page 12 shows population increase, but a chart of energy-consumption increase, increase of raw material extraction, or even the increase in the accumulation of knowledge (the sheer quantity of information now doubles every ten years*) would look just about the same.

On the **economic** side of life, the "energy explosion" is bringing us across the Great Divide into trans-civilization by tipping the scales from *scarcity* to *abundance*. In the developed countries of the world, energy is not as scarce as it once was, and so mankind is now able to do and produce more than ever before in history. Seeing this advance in the developed countries, under-developed countries around the world are doing everything they can to catch up in this march of history.

Because we are crossing the Great Divide in the economic area of life, we will soon be crossing it in the **political** area as well.

---

* (This same footnote applies to previous pages as well.) Statistics quoted from A. Toffler, "The Future as a Way of Life," HORIZON magazine, summer 1965, pp. 108-115.

We are living in the days of a "freedom explosion" taking place throughout the world. The scales are being tipped from *dependence* to *self-government*. There are conflicting ideologies as to what really is political freedom and which system is the best for attaining it, but the goal is the same: self-rule.

At the same time that individual nations are winning their independence from other nations, we are also coming to see the need of long-range steps toward the formation of a world government (since the planet is becoming more and more economically and culturally united, this is bound to require a political unity eventually). This world government will not be an *empire* as in past ages (where one people or nation ruled the others) but will hopefully be a *democracy* in some as yet uncreated form.

We have yet to cross this political Great Divide, but the first steps in the crossing are already being taken. Enlightened countries today are gradually accepting more responsibility to do what is in their power to help the various peoples of the world carry off their freedom explosion successfully and peacefully.

This political enlightenment is one effect of crossing the economic Great Divide. Formerly, when energy was a scarce commodity, one country would advance economically at the expense of other countries; today when energy is more abundantly at man's disposal, advanced countries are becoming less exploitative and more sharing in their attitude toward economically weaker countries.

In so doing we *humanize* the process of evolution, *sharing* it with all men rather than advancing at someone else's expense. We help human beings cultivate their humanness everywhere, rather than exploit human beings in one place for the advantage of a favored few in another.

In the past, the human race has advanced unevenly largely because one part of humanity exploited another part. When one civilization advanced enough in modes of travel to other civilizations in other parts of the world, a problem would arise as to what to do with the resources discovered in the more primitive people's land. A resource such as precious metal or oil or timber might be useful to the advanced civilization but not immediately useful to the more primitive one.

Throughout history, the more powerful civilizations have solved this problem in a variety of ways showing a rainbow of degrees of responsibility. In some cases they simply took possession of the more helpless peoples' land, thus depriving them of the one resource they knew how to use (hunting or farming land, as in the case of the American Indian). In other cases the more powerful civilization would leave the native people their land but hire them, or even force them, to work at extracting the resources for the advantage of the powerful (making Africans mine industrial diamonds for European countries, for example). The most extreme case is the exporting of natives as slaves. These are all various degrees of using the world's resources unevenly for a favored few, and even of making some human beings into resources for other human beings.

As the following chart shows, during the first half of the world's political history there has been a rainbow of degrees in mankind's evolution from slavery to freedom, leading us ever closer to the Great Divide yet to be crossed before trans-civilization establishes world freedom in the second half of history.

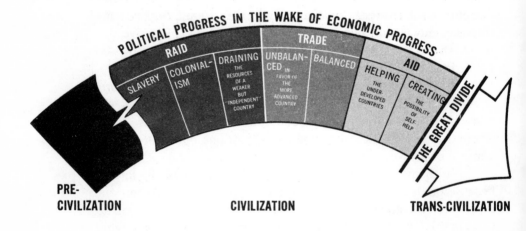

POLITICAL PROGRESS IN THE WAKE OF ECONOMIC PROGRESS

RAID — SLAVERY | COLONIALISM | DRAINING THE RESOURCES OF A WEAKER BUT "INDEPENDENT" COUNTRY

TRADE — UNBALANCED IN FAVOR OF THE MORE ADVANCED COUNTRY | BALANCED

AID — HELPING THE UNDER-DEVELOPED COUNTRIES | CREATING THE POSSIBILITY OF SELF-HELP

THE GREAT DIVIDE

PRE-CIVILIZATION   CIVILIZATION   TRANS-CIVILIZATION

What examples can you give, from our own nation's history, of these various degrees of progress toward this Great Divide?

The **cultural** features of trans-civilization are impossible to predict in detail. But its broad outlines can be foreseen. Basically the culture of trans-civilization will involve three explosions: in the area of *education,* the "knowledge explosion"; in the area of *life-style,* the "change explosion"; and in the area of *vision of life,* the "leisure explosion."

These three explosions are related. Because the quantity of information known to man doubles so rapidly, changes are always taking place. New and better ways of understanding things lead to new and better ways of doing things which means that things will be always changing; people will be moving from place to place more frequently; ideas and philosophies will be continually in flux; artists will be continually exploring new media and forms of expression; and the average work-week will have been so shortened that everyone will have more leisure time than work time and will need to find creative outlets for the use of their time.

These things are the dream. They express mankind's vision of human possibility. But they will not happen by themselves. Only men can make them happen—or fail to meet the challenge of history. *Economic* progress (from scarcity to abundance) can be channeled through *political* progress (from dependence to self-rule) for the sake of *cultural* progress (from drudgery to celebration). But such progress will not be automatic. It depends upon man's attitude toward his fellow man.

Man dying of starvation on the banks of the Ganges River in India.   FRED LEAVITT

Rude awakening

The dream of trans-civilization is a dream of the dignity of man. It is the vision of a world in which man's **economic** progress has carried him to such a point that he *no longer has to struggle with nature for survival but has tamed it for his own purposes.* Freed from this economic struggle, man's **political** progress envisions him as arriving at the point where he *no longer has to struggle with his fellow man to obtain basic human rights but receives them as his birthright.* The dream of trans-civilization is the vision of a world in which economic and political progress are the basis of a **cultural** fulfillment in which *man's chief preoccupation is not survival but celebration* (this does not mean an endless round of parties, but a deep appreciation of all the good things of life—beauty, truth, goodness, love—and the leisure time to creatively express this appreciation.

However, this dream could turn out to be a nightmare instead of a vision. The explosive force of man's progress is much like the explosive force of its symbol, atomic energy. It can be destructive as well as constructive.

In the previous chapter we sketched the *humanizing possibilities* of trans-civilization on the other side of the Great Divide. We must now take a realistic look at its *de-humanizing* possibilities. Since in this booklet we are focusing on the economic side of life, we will be examining the *economic causes of de-humanization:* in other words, the problem of **poverty.** We will look at three run-away explosions already created by economic progress, and then at the poverty they inflict on human beings.

19

The Population Explosion

The population explosion has been made possible by economic progress, especially in the field of medicine—lengthening human life, removing the causes of infant mortality, defeating once-fatal diseases, etc. But this very progress has created an opposite problem. Whereas previously there was always danger of not enough people to keep the human race self-sustaining, now there is danger of too many. We have more means than ever before for feeding, clothing, and sheltering mankind; but these very means of survival have caused so much survival that the number of persons outstrips the number of means of caring for them. At the present time, population growth is faster than economic growth.

While you are reading for the next 15 minutes, during that time 420 persons around the world will die from the effects of malnutrition. During that same time, the world's population will increase by 1,770 persons—the difference between total births and deaths.* By simple arithmetic, this means that tomorrow at this time there will be 169,920 more mouths to feed even though 40,320 have died during the same day from lack of nutrition.

According to a recent estimate, the number of people who actually starve to death (as compared to the large number of those who die from other effects of malnutrition as well) is 12,000 persons per day.** In one year's time this totals 4,380,000 people —well over the entire population of Chicago. In effect, one major city in the world starves to death every year.

Starvation is the most dramatic evidence of economic poverty in our world, but actually the proportion of persons who starve each day is slight compared to the much vaster number who manage to stay alive but always hungry, uncomfortable, and driven to desperation. A dying man is pitiful, but the man who must hang onto life only to see his children undernourished and starving is more desperate still.

---

* Figures from United Press International, as reported by Bruce W. Munn in the Chicago Sun-Times, March 26, 1967.
** Figure quoted by Sylvia Porter in the March 7, 1967 issue of the *New York Post*.

ROSCOE DRUMMOND

*Too Little Food; Too Many People**

WASHINGTON — Millions of human beings are going to be at the point of starvation during the next two decades.

The end result could be world catastrophe—and even the food-richest nation in the world, the United States, would not escape.

Today more than half of the people of the world are hungry and in less than 20 years the number of hungry people will exceed the entire present population. These are the careful conclusions of Dr. George W. Irving Jr. of the Agriculture Department.

While food is already woefully inadequate in India, Pakistan, Latin America and China, these areas of the world also face population increases that make any prospective growth in food resources a mere pittance in an accelerating calamity.

At least 70,000,000 people are being added to the world every year, increasing the use of land needed for living space and decreasing the acreage available for raising food. In Latin America alone the population will mount from 25,000,000 to 70,000,000 by the turn of the century and India will add 200,000,000 by 1980.

And what will this mean? Some unpleasantness here and there? Some suffering in the most congested parts of the world? I give you the calmly stated but dire forecast of Dr. Raymond Ewell, a vice president of State University of New York at Buffalo:

"If these trends continue for the next 10 or 15 years, mass starvation will inevitably result."

This is no minority view. This is the unanimous judgment of the specialists in the field of food and population.

The prospect of increasing food supplies to come anywhere near to catching up with mounting population is not in sight.

Because American agriculture is so productive, does this mean the United States will be immune from the effects of these twin scourges—undernourishment and overpopulation? It doesn't. Americans will not be starving by 2000, but the United States will either have to share its dwindling reserves of food or face the fury of nations and peoples driven to desperation.

If we think the cold war is a threat, the world's cold hunger and overpopulation will be a far greater peril, because the consequences of these conditions will almost certainly be political chaos on a scale we have never seen.

There are no easy answers, but we had better begin thinking, because the survival of the human race is at stake.

* Roscoe Drummond's column as published in the Chicago *Sun-Times*, March 10, 1967.

21

The urban explosion

The urban explosion has been made possible by economic progress, especially in the fields of transportation and storage—moving large quantities of food and supplies to people many miles distant from the source of supply; and storing perishables in usable condition; and also the "storage and transportation" of people in great density through sophisticated methods of housing and transit. But this very progress has created an opposite problem. Whereas previously people flocked to the city as the great center of human activity, today many people are fleeing the city as a great asphalt monster of de-humanization. We have more economic, political, and cultural resources than ever before centralized in the city; but this very implosion (inward explosion) of people and things and activities into the city has caused so much pressure that the number of problems and confusions and congestions outstrips the means of solving them.

Unless the problems of the cities are solved, the problems of the world cannot be solved—for the world is fast becoming one gigantic city.

At the time of this writing, world population grows about 2% a year, but city population grows twice that fast (4%); some of the largest cities have a population increase of 8% each year. In the year 1800 only about 2½% of the world's population lived in cities of 20,000 or more; in 1950 it was 21% of the world's population that lived in such cities. In the year 2000, when you will be in your fifties, more than one-fourth of the world will be living in *larger* cities (population of 100,000 or more); by the year 2050, more than half the world will be living in such cities.

By that time, the distinction between city and suburbs, and even between one major metropolitan region and another, will have disappeared in many places. On our East Coast, the Atlantic seaboard from Boston to Washington D.C. and beyond will have become one continuous city-strip (those who foresee this have already given it a name: *Megalopolis*). Other areas of our country, also, will have merged into city-strips. (Where do you think they will be?)

Even people who live in small towns or on farms are becoming more citified in their life-style and outlook, due to better and quicker transportation, communication, mass production, and so on. No one can escape the necessity of becoming aware of the problems and possibilities of urban living, for most young people will be moving to larger cities as they get older (while their own home town either gets larger or gets swallowed up in the enlarging boundaries of the major metropolitan area nearest by). As the rapidly dwindling farm land itself becomes more consolidated into larger co-operative farm industries, the smaller and smaller percentage of persons it takes to run these huge farm complexes will themselves be more and more influenced by the economic and political control that will emanate from cities, where voting strength and tax dollars cluster.

This process of urbanization, made possible by civilization, will be exploded into completion by trans-civilization. Civilization, extending man's power, shrank space. Trans-civilization, exploding man's power, compresses space. Civilization made the concept of one world possible; trans-civilization is making the concept of one world-city possible. Already, news can travel around the world faster than it could travel from one end of a city to another a hundred years ago.

The energy explosion, the communications explosion, the information explosion, and the population explosion—all of these are compressing people together on the planet in a complex interaction which is repeating on a world-wide scale what happened in pioneer times on a local scale—we are witnessing the birth pains of one planetary city.

The world's major cities of today are now undergoing severe growth pains. The one-world planet-city of tomorrow will undergo the same growth pains unless the problems can be solved before they reach world-wide proportions.

What about the city you live in? Or if you do not live in a city, what about the major city which dominates your region? Do you know its history? Do you know how it grew? Do you know how it is evolving this very minute? Can you name its current major problems?

While all cities have their own unique story as far as particular details go, the general pattern of most cities' growth is the same. Their original settlers found a convenient geographical location along some waterfront. Perhaps it was a harbor where boats could load and unload; perhaps it was the central spot in some vast farm region and therefore the most logical place to set up trade exchanges.

Once it is "born," a strategic city grows almost in spite of itself. The ordinary population increase due to its inhabitants' having children is amplified by outside pressures sending ever greater numbers of new in-migrants into the city. But the presence of new people demands even more new people. As one group of newcomers arrives, they need houses; to build these, construction laborers are required; to supply these, truckers and warehouses are required; to handle all these services, offices and managers and secretaries are required; these people in turn need to live and eat, and require even more houses, services, etc. Eventually the growing city becomes a kind of whirlpool requiring or inviting a constant influx of people, piling them closer and closer upon one another in ever-increasing complexity. The center of this human whirlpool is the central business district.

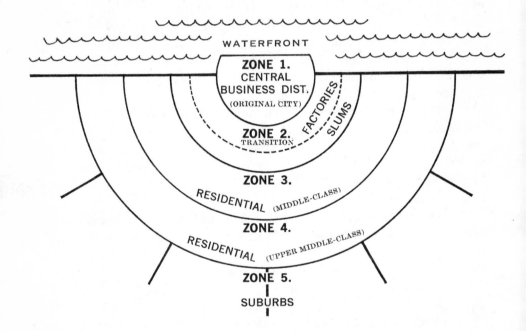

WATERFRONT

ZONE 1.
CENTRAL
BUSINESS DIST.
(ORIGINAL CITY)

FACTORIES

SLUMS

ZONE 2.
TRANSITION

ZONE 3.
RESIDENTIAL (MIDDLE-CLASS)

ZONE 4.
RESIDENTIAL (UPPER MIDDLE-CLASS)

ZONE 5.

SUBURBS

A counterpressure builds up, the need for expansion. Outward from the central business district, the city extends its boundaries. Actually today, it is more realistic to think in terms of the "urban complex" or "metropolitan area" (that is to say, the city plus its suburbs), for it is only the total metropolitan area that makes up the whole economic unit. The central business district expands, pushing back the residential sections and causing new residential areas to be built at the outskirts of the city. We

24

could "stop" a city's growth at any moment of time and take an economic cross-section of it (much as a person sawing down a tree could find a cross-section of its rings which represent various layers of growth).

Most cities of notable size have expanded in a series of "zones" which are irregular and concentric rings around the central business section of the city. The boundaries between these zones are not marked, or course, and they can't be pinned down exactly. Moreover, they are always changing as the city expands and buildings of one type are reconverted or torn down and replaced by another type. But the general pattern can be simplified and represented by the chart on page 24.

The diagram above, of course, is an oversimplification; it represents the "theoretical" waves of a city's growth. In actuality, the five zones are more irregular due to unique factors of each city's geographical history. The three major factors which modify this wave of expansion are:

Waterways. If the city was born around the junction of waterways, the business and factory zones tend to spread along the fingers of water, with the zones of expansion fanning around this pattern.

Railroads. Railroads, built extensively to serve the heavily industrialized waterway zones and branching off from there, tend to extend the factory zone around themselves.

The Auto. Automobiles made the population mobile— people no longer depended on mass transport but could move speedily in and out of the congested city at will.

"The suburbs are essentially a post-World War II phenomenon. Until 1940, successive census showed consistent population increases in the city proper. Then came the long-sustained upward sweep in personal income which characterized the forties and fifties. The desire for space, apparently latent in almost all city dwellers, was translated into a massive outward migration. People enjoyed better incomes, they bought automobiles, and the resulting move to the suburbs meant that population growth in many central cities slowed appreciably. Some cities . . . actually declined in population."*

A metropolitan area's wave of expansion runs roughly as follows: as the central business district expands with the addition

---

* *Metropolis,* ed. C. E. Elias et al. (Belmont: Wadsworth, 1964), p. 61.

of more factories, offices, stores, and related services, it is the people who live in zone 2 who are constantly uprooted. Those who can afford to, move out to zone 3, whose inhabitants in turn, if they can afford it, move out to zones 4 and 5.

As cities grow, their growing pains become most acute in economic "zone 2." It is in this area of most metropolitan regions that **slums** *are born.*

> The slum . . . is an area of high land values but cheap rents. This curious contradiction is the result of such land being held "in pawn," so to speak, on the assumption that the central business district will expand into the area and will bring its business firms, manufacturing establishments, and high-priced rental units such as hotels and apartment hotels. The landowners, who seldom live in the area, do not wish to improve the slum housing since it will eventually be torn down. This fact and the rather undesirable location make for cheap rentals.*

In the early days of a city, the slum area was a place where newcomers could find cheap housing to make a temporary stopover while they were looking for a job or while building their incomes. Then, in the days of massive immigration into our country, there was no place for the vast numbers of immigrants to go but to these less desirable portions of the city where they crowded together with relatives, friends and compatriots from the "old country." Gradually, in a generation or two, many of these nationality groups were able to work their way higher up the economic ladder and move out to zones 3 and 4.

Today, however, there are vast numbers of persons who cannot find employment, or whose employment provides less than minimum adequate wages, so that they cannot afford to live elsewhere than in zone 2:

> Each big city in the United States has an economic underworld. And often enough this phrase is a literal description: it refers to the kitchens and furnace rooms that are under the city; it tells of the place where tens of thousands of hidden people labor at impossible wages. Like the underworld of crime, the economic underworld is out of sight, clandestine.
>
> The workers . . . are . . . denied coverage by the Minimum-Wage Law of 1961. . . . In the most recent Government figures, for example, hotel workers averaged $47.44 a week,

---

* Marshall B. Clinard, "Deviant Behavior, Urban-Rural Contrasts," in *Metropolis,* ed. C. E. Elias et al. (Belmont: Wadsworth, 1964), p. 242.

laundry workers $46.45, general-merchandise employees $48.37, and workers in factories making work clothing $45.58. . . .

They are cheated by crooked unions; they are used by racketeers.*

So it happens that those whose economic *needs* are the greatest are forced to live where *conditions* are poorest.

> In this six-story building, converted into furnished rooms, filth prevails throughout—filled garbage cans without covers line the hallways with the surplus refuse spilling over; roaches and rats abound; broken flooring, plumbing, windows, lighting fixtures and plaster are observable throughout. The average room size (occupied by a family) is 13 x 15 with two beds, a dresser, two chairs, a table, a refrigerator and a closet, as the standard equipment supplied by the landlord. One community kitchen is used by seven families. Twelve toilets are intermittently in service on six floors. There is no lock on the door from the street and vagrants, including drug addicts and alcoholics, often wander in to sleep in the unlocked kitchens and bathrooms. This is the abode of thirty families and 105 children.**

The Cybernation Explosion

"Cybernation" is a recently coined word. It is a combination of the two words "automation" and "cybernetics" (the science of computers). It means, quite literally, *computerized automation*. It is efficiency carried to the ultimate. Automation replaces routine human muscle-work with machines; cybernetics replaces routine human mental work with computers. Cybernation replaces both the mind and muscle of man by doing the kind of routine work that would otherwise require many man-hours—and does it more speedily, more accurately, and more abundantly.

---

* Michael Harrington, *The Other America* (Baltimore: Penguin paperback, 1963), pp. 28-29.
** Dumpson, James R., "The Human Side of Urban Renewal", *The Welfarer*, Oct. 1960, pp. 1, 4.

The cybernation explosion has been made possible by economic progress, especially in the field of technology. Its basic gift to man is that it frees human minds and bodies from routine tasks for more creative ones. But this very progress has created an opposite problem. Whereas previously there was more work to do than men available to do it, uncontrolled cybernation is today creating a work vacuum. Man foresees the time when he will have more leisure than he will know what to do with (unless his basic education is enlarged from training-for-work to initiation-into-creative-leisure). More serious a problem (at least at the present time) is that many men have been pushed out of their jobs entirely by machines and have no available alternate means of employment—no means of supporting themselves and their families. Intermediate between these two problems is a third, the problem of men who have enough work to do but whose work is so routine that they are literally appendages of the machines they run. The designers of machines and the managers of cybernated industries may indeed be freed by the machines for more creative tasks, but those who actually run or feed the machines are in fact left with tasks less creative than what the machines themselves have been designed to do.

The remedy is not to halt the cybernation explosion, but to channel it and pace its progress in accord with human dignity. At the present time we are just beginning to discover the ways to do this; the promise of controlled cybernation is there, but the threat of its uncontrolled advance is all too real.

For all three runaway explosions (the population explosion, the urban explosion, and the cybernation explosion) there is no possibility of reversing the trend. The world will have more people, not fewer; more cities, not fewer; more computerized mechanical services, not less. We have the theoretical possibility of feeding more people than the earth now supports—but we must still discover how to tap our resources on their behalf; cybernation can help us do this but we must still discover how to direct it to world-wide needs rather than merely short-range advantages of immediate profit to this or that industry; the massive co-operation and interaction which will enable the human race to co-ordinate these efforts cannot be secured unless the trend toward world citification continues—but only if we learn how to make our cities more livable, not less so.

In other words, the three explosions are interconnected. The problems of one cannot be solved except in relation to the problems of the others. The economic progress of civilization has created the problems and the economic, political and cultural tools of civilization must provide the means of solving them. But mankind is involved in a race against time. At the present time, problems are beginning to outstrip solutions. The dream of trans-civilization is in danger of becoming a nightmare.

ORLANDO CABANBAN

The nightmare
of poverty

The goal of economic progress, pushing civilization forward into trans-civilization, is to make man rich—rich not in a shortsighted, merely economic sense, but rich in such a way that his *economic* well-being is at the service of his *political* freedom to pursue *cultural* ends that truly enrich his spirit.

But human progress does not advance uniformly at all times and in all places. Certain persons or small groups (and certain countries) are usually in a specially advantaged position, the first to benefit from a breakthrough. Behind their vanguard advance into human dignity, the rest of the human race hopes to follow; but the massive uplifting of the entire human race is a gigantic task which, in the past at least, has required centuries. There has always been in the world, up to now, an economic lag between the rich and the poor; a political lag between the free and the exploited; a cultural lag between the skilled and the unskilled, the learned and the unlearned, the creative and the unfulfilled.

Time is running out on these lags, however. Today the rich and the poor, the free and the chained, the educated and the potentially talented are rubbing elbows in a world unified as never before by transportation, communications media, and economic interdependence. Those in the rear of civilization's progress will no longer wait centuries to catch up; they want to catch up *now* —for they fear that the "progress explosion" is accelerating so fast that unless they can catch up now they may never be able to.

Ours is the age of transition, the age of decision. Today, while civilization is only just beginning to give birth to trans-civilization there is still time to decide whether trans-civilization will be made a dream for all, or a dream for some and a night-mare for others.

Poverty in the United States

This problem of economic inequality is worldwide; in the brief space available, we will look closely at its existence in our own country.

In the United States, we pride ourselves on the belief that "in our country no one starves." While this belief is probably true or nearly true, it does not tell the whole story. It gives the illusion that all is well. Here, however, is the condition of life that many Americans are forced to live in. It is the transcript of an interview with a mother of five children:*

"Don't ask me how you survive when the money stops coming in. That's what I wants to know. But I can tell ya what ya cuts down on first.

"We had this house full at Christmas time. Folks was good. Now it's all run out. But it gave the kids an uplift and they been smiling ever since. So we thanks God we got that left, their smiles.

"The first things folks can cut down on are gas and lights. Ya puts more clothes on and I even saved $5 one month by using oil lamps.

"But ya really should have one 40 watt light bulb in the house to read and see by. The rest can be 25 watt bulbs. And it's a sin to burn a light during the day. Most of the poor people don't know about this. I went into one house that had a 75 watt bulb burning and they even had to use a shade.

"And you can turn your refrigerator off at night if you ain't got any perishable meats in it.

---

* From *They Speak for Themselves: Interviews with the Destitute of Chicago*, as told to Kenan Heise (Chicago: Young Christian Workers, 1965), pp. 17-19.

31

"We use gas and that's expensive. But the gas company is good. They shut off the heat and I goes downstairs and turns it back on. They know me.

"The biggest items are food and clothes. Ya can't get around 'em.

"I've heard that one green onion is worth a whole plate of anything else. So we cuts up an onion and puts it over rice or potatoes. Or you can cut out the vegetable if you got canned fruit, cuz they counts the same. Mainly, we fills 'em up on potatoes or rice or spaghetti or corn bread. You don't feed 'em potatoes and corn bread at the same meal like some people I know. And the rich people even have a salad and vegetable at the same meal and that ain't necessary for nobody.

"The cheapest meat I can get are lambs breasts. They sell for 21 cents a pound. Sometimes chicken is 21 cents a pound, but usually it's around 29 cents. We buy it when it's low.

"Milk is 89 cents a gallon. Larry here, after you give him all the milk he wants, he goes back and steals the rest. When we got money, we give 'em milk. We give 'em enough milk to fill up on. I think you should give 'em enough milk to give 'em a good washing out with it. Then you don't have enough for milk for a week or two. But I think that's the best way. Cuz if you can't give it to 'em regular, you should give 'em enough to wash 'em out with it.

"We work all summer to beat the watermelon rap. We buy it from the grocery store instead of the trucks. It only cost 49 cents ice cold at the store.

"You can get pretty good buys on clothes at Goodwill, if you got a car and can shop around at them. But I've had this broken leg and couldn't get around.

"You can get a $12 pair of shoes second-handed for $2.50, but them is what you really got to shop for.

"Ain't none of these kids right now got any underwear at all. I can get a 70 cent undershirt for a kid for 20 cents at Goodwill. Dresses are 75 cents to $1.00. A woman's dress is the best thing to buy for a child or a little girl cuz it's got the best material in it. All you got to do is cut it down and you got a real good dress.

"Used to be 10 or 12 years ago that ya could make $6 or $7 a day junking. You'd always see women baby-buggy junking. But a lot of men have made a great big business out of it now. Now the winos collect all the junk. Let me guarantee you there aint' no junk in this neighborhood. People ain't got it to throw out. Now you got to go way out. You know, where they got farms and things.

"And there ain't nothing left you can sell. I pawned my diamond rings, my guitar and my radio down on Madison street several years ago. I worked for years to buy those.

"It'd cost us $15 to get the TV fixed, but I think TV has caused more backsliding than whiskey.

"You can get by but you can't survive. The welfare is really hard on people that can't spend money wisely and I don't blame them. But the children suffer.

"For entertainment, we all go to church."

How many persons in the United States are economically poor? That depends on what you mean by "poor." We are constantly being deluged with statistics compiled by government agencies and other social researchers, and sometimes their figures seem to conflict, unless we realize that they are based on different standards of what it means to be "poor." The following threefold definition is given by the U.S. Government:*

Minimum comfort. For a family of four, it is estimated that it would cost $5500 per year to maintain themselves in living conditions which would substantially take care of their physical needs but would not allow them the ordinary blessings which the average middle-class American citizen takes for granted. (For a family of less than four people, the income necessary for "minimum comfort" would be correspondingly less.) In the United States today there are *70 million* people who cannot afford a life of minimum comfort.

Minimum adequacy. If the same family of four had an income of only $3500 per year, they would be able to survive but would be in constant poor health because of inadequate diet, clothing, and shelter. Of the 70 million mentioned above, *46 million people* in our country are living on a minimum-adequacy budget or less.

Minimum subsistence. Of those, *20 million people* are living on a budget which is the equivalent of $2500 or less per year for a family of four. These people are those hungry, sick, discouraged ones who just barely survive if at all.

Forty to fifty million Americans are *invisible* to their more abundantly blessed fellow men, because they cannot afford to live in the more prosperous areas; because their clothes (being com-

---

* The figures are subject to variation as the cost of living rises.

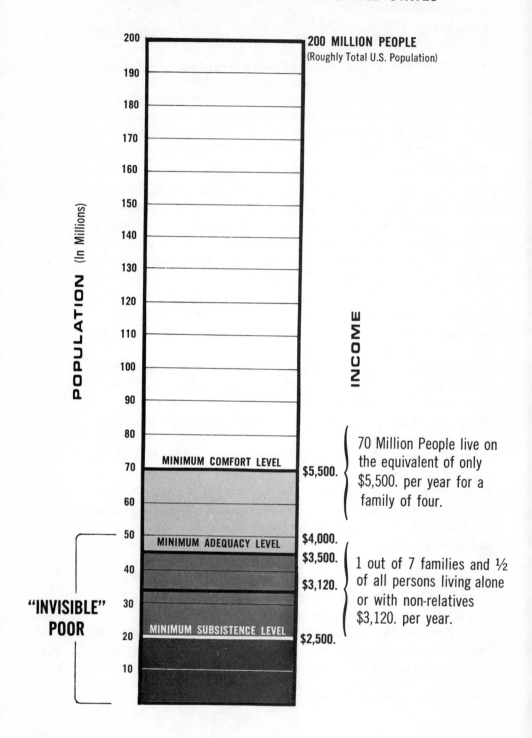

ECONOMIC DISTRIBUTION IN THE UNITED STATES

POPULATION (In Millions)

INCOME

200 — **200 MILLION PEOPLE** (Roughly Total U.S. Population)

MINIMUM COMFORT LEVEL — $5,500.

70 Million People live on the equivalent of only $5,500. per year for a family of four.

MINIMUM ADEQUACY LEVEL — $4,000.

$3,500.

$3,120.

1 out of 7 families and ½ of all persons living alone or with non-relatives $3,120. per year.

MINIMUM SUBSISTENCE LEVEL — $2,500.

"INVISIBLE" POOR

mon enough thanks to American mass production) do not reveal the sacrifices they make in food, shelter, and other necessities; because many of them are old and do not get around much; because they are unable to find employment and thus are not seen in places where well-paid people work; and/or because they do not have the political power that goes with education, organization, and money. Though we are told about them in statistics from time to time, they do not really stay in our minds.

They are hidden from the advertising pages, shop windows, social columns, and public imagination. The scene is taken by the favored few:

> How much does it cost to be really well-dressed? The ladies picked as "America's Best-Dressed Women" spend an average of $50,000 a year on clothes—some as much as $100,000. The bulk of the money goes for furs and jewelry and original designs by French and Italian couturiers. It also includes such items as handmade underwear, $100 shoes, $500 handbags, etc.*

The Poverty Culture

Just as true riches are more than economic, so poverty is more than merely economic privation. Just as economic well-being supports political freedom and together with it makes it possible to cultivate one's talents in the pursuit of a meaningful human life, so the reverse is also true: *economic powerlessness makes one a prey to political powerlessness, and these two together drastically limit one's opportunity for the culture of a more than rudimentary human living.*

In this section we will look through an economic lens at the barriers to human fulfillment which people have to struggle with when they have been left behind in economic progress. Some persons are so poor in the economic category that political freedom is meaningless or impossible for them, and their cultural vision of life is limited to a bare level of humanness because their daily preoccupation is a constant anxiety for survival.

---

* *Parade* Magazine, Feb. 19, 1967.

ORLANDO CABANBAN

The description will be basically that of poverty in the slums of large American cities, but its implications are more wide-ranging. It is true that rural poverty is not exactly the same as urban poverty, but the differences are variations on a theme rather than fundamental depth-differences. It is also true that poverty in other countries is somewhat different in style from American poverty. But limitations of time and space require us to concentrate on American urban poverty.

Since the entire world is becoming urbanized and Westernized in its technology (though it will probably eventually be Easternized and Africanized in its culture) the style of poverty in other societies will more and more approximate that of urban poverty in our own society as trans-civilization enlarges city economic problems to planetsize scale.

Understanding your own major city today is the best starting point for understanding the world-city you and your children will inhabit tomorrow. Taking responsibility for your own major city is the first step in creating tomorrow's world-city as a place of maximum human possibility—before economic, political, and cultural conflicts (if left unleashed) create the planet into an asphalt and steel chaos more uninhabitable than any jungle.

In the analysis which follows, you might find it worthwhile to read with red pen in hand, marking each item with an E or P or C to denote which of the three aspects of society it refers to; and mentally noting how the political and cultural problems can be in some way related to the economic side of man's life.)

There is a difference between short-term economic hardship and long-term "poverty." The first is a condition which can befall anyone if fortune takes a bad turn for him; it is also the condition of many professional people when they are young and just starting out in their career—such as many medical students, lawyers, school teachers, etc. This condition does not create a "poverty culture" because it does not carry with it the inevitability of a closed future.

By contrast, there is that economic condition which puts a person or family near the bottom of the socio-economic ladder and offers little or no hope of possibility for rising above it. This is true of many unskilled laborers, or laborers whose one skill is no longer needed (for example, coal miners in a town where the mines have just shifted to automation, laying off hundreds or thousands of men who now have no other means of livelihood, and who then drift to larger cities with no particular skill to offer on the labor market.)

Poverty creates poverty. Those who miss out on the opportunities which human living offers for the more fortunate, thereby live out a style of human existence which, utilizing fewer possibilities, in its turn creates fewer possibilities or at least the expectation of fewer possibilities. This creates a "poverty mind"—a despair which breeds its own problems.

Poverty of this kind is passed on from generation to generation. Parents, living in an atmosphere of despair, worried about their children's hunger and deprivation, portray to the all-seeing eye of these children the hopeless bleakness of their lives. Their children soon learn by osmosis that life is an empty round of dead hours punctuated by momentary diversions and—once in a while—the surprise windfall of an odd job.

The culture of poverty can be studied cross-sectionally by looking at the following areas of life which express and continue that culture: education, ambition, health and life style, unemployment, exploitability, and crime.

1) **Education.**

a) *environmental.* The culture of poverty is not merely one of the *absence* of economic and social possibility; it is also one of the *presence* of despair, futility, and unworthiness by contrast with public status symbols. Thus, children in a poverty culture are not only *behind* other children their own age in educable readiness when they reach school age, but they are subconsciously *influenced against* such readiness. The values and possibilities officially held by the school and personally lived by the teachers are already rejected by the children who come to the schools and teachers. They already feel themselves to be "outside" the system; they feel that what they are being taught could only be useful to the "insiders" of society, who already "have it made."

b) *school.* While more and better education is needed in poverty-culture areas, the tragedy is that the schools and other institutions which ought to be serving these special needs are usually understaffed, underfinanced, and underadapted. In spite of a few heroically dedicated teachers, by and large teachers do not generally like to teach in such schools because of the nearly overwhelming difficulties involved. The result is that beginning or experienced-but-inferior teachers, appear in higher proportion in these schools, often assigned there unwillingly. The kind of education they give, instead of remedying the culture of poverty, in many ways reinforces it. The children sense this kind of teacher's resentment, rejection, and lack of respect for them; the children are reinforced in their own lack of self-respect as well as lack of respect for "the establishment."

2) **Ambition.** The poverty culture lowers one's level of ambition from long-range goals to goals which can be achieved today or tomorrow.

a) *Delayed gratification.* Persons for whom the future promises possibility are able to maintain themselves in long-term disciplines of work, study, and cultivation of social skills and graces, making sacrifices in the present moment for the sake of greater enjoyment and achievement in the future. But persons whose future holds no such promise see it as nothing more than the continuation of the present life they know now; they see no point in delaying their gratifications but limit themselves to those which can be obtained or achieved with a minimum of effort, money, or time. With this kind of a habitual outlook on life, they tend to think of themselves as unable to make long-term use of things like money or education if they come their way. They cannot imagine a cultivation of these precious resources, but fritter them away in the present moment. Education is slighted, not taken seriously. Money is used to satisfy immediate needs and celebrated away in a flash rather than invested in the future.

b) *Sense of time.* Middle-class people tend to think of time as a schedule—punctually divided into appointments and routines which are faithfully held to. Poverty-acculturated people, on the other hand, tend to think of time as the present moment without precise units of responsibility. They find it hard to be punctual and organized because there is no point in it. The "gratification" of knowing that one is proceeding gradually toward a delayed gratification does not enter their imagination.

c) *Self-concept.* When life does not seem to hold many possibilities, there is not much call for the emergence and flowering of each person's unique personality. The usual identifiers of name, face, and family tradition are missing. Teachers in Head-Start Programs, for example, sometimes find young children who do not know their own names or even know that they have a name. (They are addressed as "You" or "Boy" at home.) In these programs even a mirror is a useful teaching tool for these youngsters, since many do not have mirrors at home and don't know what they look like. The personal relationships at home are so simple and elemental that there is rarely a need for complete sentences to be spoken at home. Thus, such children become confused and cry when a sentence is spoken to them at school because such a complicated expression is too bewildering for their unaccustomed minds.

Living in such a careless environment, they are careless of themselves. Many poorly dressed children do not tie their shoe or sneaker laces, and many of them do not close what buttons they do have on their coats even if the weather is cold and they are shivering! They have many accidents and fires simply because "they do not take care." Slum children seldom really look before they run into the street, and often their parents neglect them horribly and leave dangerous objects like matches about or let them perch at open windows or on fire-escapes.

3) **Health and life style.** People who live in a poverty culture suffer not only the absence of necessities but the presence of atrocities, all of which tend to degrade the human spirit:

a) *overcrowdedness* of one's neighborhood, house, and room which leads to lack of essential privacy in personal relationships.

b) *lack of facilities* such as heating, light, fresh air, play space, books, writing materials, musical instruments.

c) *inhuman sanitary conditions* including rats, bugs, inadequate toilet facilities, dirty kitchens, glass and dirt and garbage in the streets, torn, dirty clothing, and diseases and illnesses.

d) *unhealthy human influences pervading the atmosphere*, such as alcoholism, dope and drug addiction, sexual excess, broken home situations and absence of a father, and a high frequency of neurotic and psychotic personality disorders.

e) *impersonal or even degrading treatment by* absentee landlords, absentee store owners, police, school system, and welfare agencies.

4) **Unemployment.** The poor are generally less able to find employment than others, for the following reasons:

a) Their *poverty of education* leaves them with few if any skills, which are less and less needed anyway as automation takes over.

b) Their *poverty of ambition* leaves them without motivation to learn on the job what would enable them to rise in it, or to take training in new skills.

40

c) Their *lack of awareness of the larger society* keeps them ignorant of social agencies which could help them find better jobs.

d) *Jobs with no future* are often the only kind they can begin with; such jobs furthermore do not pay enough to enable them to afford more schooling or even do not allow them the days off necessary to go job-hunting for better jobs.

e) *Racial or ethnic minority groups* are often segregated from equal employment opportunities.

f) *Inadequate public transportation* exists in the slums of many cities, where the very poor are unable to afford private transportation to areas where better-paying jobs might be available.

g) *Many of the poor are aged or aging,* and are selected out by employment screening processes. Many others are mothers with absent, deceased, or non-existent husbands; such mothers, usually with *large families of growing children,* are unable to leave home to find employment.

h) *Growing up in a mother-dominated family structure* where the tradition is one of masculine irresponsibility or economic impotency, the male self-image of growing boys is so degraded that only the most heroic are able to find within themselves the attitudes of responsibility and perseverance that are necessary for job-finding and job-keeping.

5) **Exploitability.** The poor are easy to exploit, as many unprincipled persons who take advantage of them have learned. Exploitation of the poor takes on many *forms,* such as:

a) high prices for poor housing;
b) upped prices at stores;
c) unfair installment payments;
d) illegally high interest rates on loans;
e) shoddy materials, food, liquor, cars, clothes;
f) unfair wages and labor practices;
g) intimidation.

The *reasons* why the poor can be so easily exploited include the following:

a) The poor are generally less educated.
b) They are more desperate (hence easy prey for loan sharks, door-to-door installment gougers).
c) They are often fixed to their location and thus a captive market for upped store prices.
d) They are more prone than others to accept shoddy merchandise.

41

e) They have less recourse to legal machinery and institutions, either because they cannot afford them or because they are unaware of their legal rights.

f) They have almost no political power to organize for higher wages, better city services, etc.

6) **Crime.** The crime rate in poverty-culture areas of the city is greater than in other areas, because of:

a) economic desperation

b) generalized sense of revenge:
1) towards affluent society—"we deserve it from them"
2) towards own neighbors—"they'd steal from me so I steal first"

c) example of crime while growing up: older brothers and sisters, parents, neighborhood heroes.

d) negative attitude toward police and other authority figures:
1) if get away with it, an outsmarter
2) if caught, a martyr.

e) unhealthy human relationship patterns including alcoholism and neurotic patterns intensified by too-close living conditions lead to higher incidence of anger, generally violent behavior, and even murder.

f) larger number of school dropouts, unemployed and unemployable with free time and no constructive outlets.

g) gang and syndicate structures.

Minority Group Poverty

Nobody wants to be poor. However, civilization's economic progress has not yet been extended to everyone. Scarcity has not yet given way to abundance for everyone.

In the scramble to obtain a sufficient share of this world's goods, some persons are in a more advantageous position than others. They have been launched into adult life with sufficient education to earn a comfortable living, to participate intelligently in the political processes which are theirs as citizens of a free country, and to profit from the cultural opportunities which are available to those who appreciate them.

Yet there are many others who have not been launched into life with these advantages. Lacking a solid economic base, their parents were not able to afford for them the kind of education that could free them; lacking this education they are unable to take advantage of economic or political opportunities, for they are either unaware of them or unqualified or outclassed by those who compete with them for jobs or services.

Being in a disadvantageous starting position is not merely an individual matter, but it is often a group matter. Often it happens that one's nationality group or one's geographical region has a history which places the whole group at a disadvantage, so that a member of that group would have to be very exceptional, or luckier than average, in order to compensate for the head start which members of other groups have.

In the United States today there are many minority groups which, for reasons of history, now find themselves at an economic, political, and cultural disadvantage which causes them to fall further and further behind the progress of society. We will briefly describe five such groups.

1) **Newcomers to the continental United States.** Newcomers to the States today, because of their language problem, and if they are unskilled or of limited skill, are forced to find jobs at the lowest rung of the economic ladder. The largest group of newcomers to this continent at the present time are Spanish-speaking.

2) **Migrant farm workers.** There are thousands of families in the United States today who have no fixed home, but continually move from State to State, following the agricultural seasons. The whole family works in the fields of small farms or large farm systems for extremely low wages. Their living conditions are rudimentary—shacks without running water, screening, adequate heating or good roofing, etc. Education of their children is rudimentary, also, for their children are never in one place long enough to stay in a single school system or program, and their education often terminates at 8th grade or earlier. Thus they are not equipped to leave migrant farm work when they grow up, but are trapped in their way of life. It has been difficult, perhaps impossible, in the past for them to organize into unions because: a) being mobile and transient, organized unification is hard to establish and maintain; b) since they move from State to State, they cannot

Before king Terry began to laugh
a little. I have it! he said.
I have it!
Then Terry called the others.
Mother! he cried. angela! Kathy

benefit from uniform labor legislation nor do they have congressional representatives who recognize them as constituents; c) the varying situations in each locale where they move to work do not have uniform problems with uniform solutions.

3) **Appalachians.** Appalachia is the region of our country which comprises the Appalachian Mountain Range and its foothills. The region crosses 11 states, ranging from southern New York to northern Alabama and Georgia.

This area was settled during colonial years and afterward by pioneers who carved their own farms out of the wilderness. While railroads and highways were connecting various other parts of the United States, this mountainous region remained relatively isolated from such contacts, since the terrain discouraged railroad and highway routes.

When the United States began to become industrialized, the timber industries and coal mining industries came to Appalachia. Finding these mountaineers unaware of the tremendous value of their resources, industry agents were able to buy huge tracts of forests and coal veins for extremely low prices.

As population in the area expanded beyond what farming alone could support, more and more Appalachians were hired by mining and forestry companies. Then, when these industries became mechanized and even automated, thousands of their former workers were laid off, but were unable to return to farming because many of the streams had become polluted by mine wastes and much of the land had been ruined by strip-mining which cuts away the topsoil.

This extensive layoff, plus the inability of the remaining farmland to support an ever-increasing population, have been among the major factors making Appalachia today largely a region of poverty and depression.

As a result, hundreds of thousands of Appalachians have moved into the nation's large cities looking for jobs. Upon arriving in the big cities, many cannot find or afford other than slum housing. And, being accustomed to an individualistic free-wheeling life-style arising from their pioneer heritage, they are uneducated to the complexities which make up city life. The impersonal ways of agencies and institutions and hiring practices are something they are not prepared to cope with, as a result many of them cannot find or do not adjust to regularly paying jobs.

4) **The American Indians.** Circumstances of history have

made these ancient possessors of our land wards of the federal government. At the present time many an American Indian who leaves the economic and cultural confinement of reservation life finds in the big city that his lack of skills and lack of education in the sense and style of larger American life place him at the same disadvantage as other groups at the bottom of the city's socio-economic ladder.

5) **American Negroes.** All of our large cities, and many other cities and towns, are receiving a continuous influx of Negroes from the South. These persons come generally to escape two pressures: aggressive segregation, and lack of employment. Many of them also come from bankrupt farms or newly-automated farms in the rural South, bringing a minimum amount of education and little or no technical skill.

Upon arriving in the city, they are faced with economic conditions not much better than those they left behind, although the statistics of possibility are somewhat less loaded against them in the city than elsewhere.

If they come from Southern cities to Northern cities they face segregation, in more hypocritical and hardly less cruel forms than the forms they faced previously. They find that the only place in the city where they will be accepted as residents is in the slums —and not just anywhere in the slums, but only in those sections that have already "gone Negro," or in borderline neighborhoods about to "change." These sections are already overcrowded, and patterns of exploitation are already well established. The possibilities for improvement of the neighborhood have pretty well vanished, too. Schools in the area are under-staffed and underfinanced, for example. Rent tends to be higher than in other slum areas, because Negroes have no choice but to pay these rates since they cannot move to cheaper areas on account of segregation. Food prices are actually higher than in the suburbs, and often the food sold at these higher prices is stale or left over from suburban grocers. Overcrowding in the houses and underprovision of playgrounds, make for frustrating conditions of play that lead to the formation of gangs with destructive tendencies.

When citing statistics on poverty, the portion of Negro families receiving incomes below a particular figure, e.g. $3000, is often compared with the portion of white families receiving incomes below $3000. Such comparisons implicitly assume the Negro's $3000 buys as much as the white's $3000. It does not.

46

American cities have two housing markets: the city-wide white market and the circumscribed Negro market. . . . "Non-white renters and home owners obtain fewer standard quality dwellings and frequently less space than do whites paying the same amounts." . . .

Poor urban Negroes also pay more than whites for identical consumer durables bought on credit. . . .

Poor Negro families average a half person larger than poor white families. . . .

Urban renewal . . . seems to effect a net reduction in housing for poor Negroes . . . Because many urban Negroes live in slums, 60 per cent of the persons dispossessed by urban renewal demolition have been Negroes. . . . Time must elapse between demolition of old and dedication of new buildings. . . . Poor whites may move elsewhere; poor Negroes must face reduced supply.*

It is important to realize that the above description does not apply to all Negroes (for there are a growing number who, in spite of obstacles, or because of specially favorable circumstances, have been able to obtain a good education and take places in middle-class society); yet the majority still find the door of opportunity largely closed to them.

The usual characteristics of the poverty culture can be found in slums where Negroes live, just as they can be found in any other slums. But Negroes find themselves more trapped in these conditions as a group than any other group, because their obvious physical features make them more easily identifiable and hence a more ready target for being "selected out" of competitive opportunities.

Negroes who have personally risen above the conditions of poverty culture are often not given a chance to prove themselves in a talent-demanding job, or in a higher-income neighborhood, but they are treated as if their skin color automatically carried with it all the undesirable characteristics which are really caused by economic, political, and cultural factors that have no connection with skin color at all.

And those who have fallen victim to the poverty culture are treated as if this were their "natural" condition, whereas members

---

* Alan Batchelder, "Poverty: The Special Case of the Negro," *Poverty in America*, ed. Louis A. Ferman (Ann Arbor: U. of Michigan Press, 1965), pp. 113-115.

of other races whose condition of life is the same are more sympathetically interpreted and more hope is held out to them.

Thus, it has happened, more by accident of history than by any real "natural" connection, that the American Negro has become a world symbol of poverty in a rich country. To the ordinary conditions and effects of poverty are added the indignity of irrational discrimination. The poor and hungry of the world look to America, the "land of promise," and interpret the poverty of the majority of American Negroes as indicative of America's unconscious practical principles: "Since there have to be some poor people in the world, we might as well select for this position those who can be easily identified and kept at the bottom of the ladder as being their 'natural' position."

THE PEOPLE
OF GOD

The finger of God

Prophecy and Current Events

The Finger of God in History

Daniel

5:1 Once upon a time
King Belshazzar threw a banquet for a thousand noblemen,
and drank wine in front of the thousand.

2 In his drunkenness he commanded
that the gold and silver chalices
which his father Nabuchodonosor had robbed
from the Temple in Jerusalem
should be brought out for the king and his noblemen
and their wives and mistresses to drink out of.

4 They drank wine and gave toasts in honor of their idols
of gold, silver, brass, iron, wood, and stone.

5 Suddenly, next to a wall torch,
the fingers of a man's hand magically appeared,
writing on the palace wall . . .

6 The king's face turned pale and his mind reeled;
his legs trembled and his knees began to knock.

8 All the king's wise men came in
but they could not interpret the writing for the king.

13 Then Daniel the prophet was summoned in before the king.

17 Daniel told him . . .

23 "You have lifted yourself up against the Lord of heaven
and chalices from his Temple have been brought to you . . .

51

and you have sung hymns to deaf and dumb idols . . .
But the God who holds your breath in His hand,
you have ignored.
²⁴ So He has sent the hand to write . . .
²⁶ *"God has numbered the days of your kingdom*
and put an end to it."
²⁷ . . . *"You have been weighed on the scale*
and judged lacking."
²⁸ . . . *"Your kingdom is divided*
and given to the Medes and Persians."
³⁰ That same night,
Belshazzar the Chaldean King was assassinated.

Our Jewish ancestors had a gift for interpreting history. For them, nothing happened without a meaning. Everything that happened contained a message for them. Poetically they described the Unpicturable Reality behind the scenes of life as The Finger of God.

Today, as then, when sensitive men are inspired to see what is happening in their times, and point out what it means and where it is going, these prophets are for us The Finger of God.

As we feast on the plenty of the richest country in the world, the handwriting on the wall comes to us in the form of newspaper headlines or TV documentaries about international crises, riots in the slums, revolutions against regimes claimed to be unfair, threats against the "have" nations by "have-not" nations. Can we see the hand of God writing the prophecy, *God has numbered the days of your kingdom and put an end to it?*

The Finger of God plays no favorites, points at no one nation to the exclusion of others, shields no one from the threat of nuclear war. It points to the whole globe and says, *You have been weighed on the scale and judged lacking.*

What should be one world, one brotherhood of mankind, is in fact divided into armies chanting "we want" lined up against armies replying "you won't get." The handwriting of God is plainly interpreted—*Your kingdom is divided.*

But The Finger of God points not primarily to blame but to lead. Reality's most sensitive spokesmen, the prophets, point out impending destruction not because God wants us to destroy ourselves but because He wants us to foresee the coming destruction and avoid it.

THE FINGER OF GOD POINTS TO THE CITY

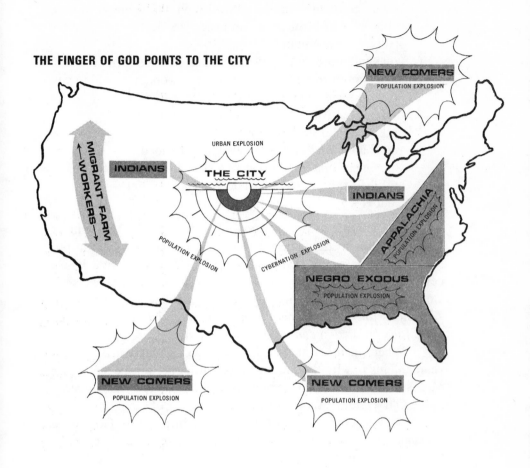

. . . . . **The Finger of God not only points out problems but carves out solutions.** As our Old Testament Bible poetically records it, it was The Finger of God which carved out in tablets of stone on Mount Sinai the social legislation which enabled the Jewish community to care for its poor:

Deuteronomy
15:4 There shall be no poor man among you.

1 Every seventh year you shall cancel all debts,

2 in this fashion: every creditor shall release
what he had lent to his neighbor.

He shall not demand it back from his neighbor—his brother

—because it is the year of the Lord's cancellation of debts.

7 In the land which the Lord your God will have given you,
if one of your brothers living inside the city
shall be a poor man,
you shall not harden your heart nor close your hand.

12 When your brother, a Hebrew man or woman, is sold to you
and has served you six years,
in the seventh year you shall let him go free;*

13 and when you send him out free,
you shall not let him go away empty-handed.

15 Remember that you also were a slave in the land of Egypt,
and the Lord your God made you free.
That is why I give you this present command.

The Church as the collective Finger of God. The "Finger of God" is our poetic name for the active presence of God in human affairs. Believing that God is the Creator of all that is, we believe that He acts *through* His creatures. Believing that He is the Creator of man's freedom, we believe that He acts *through* men. *The more fully we co-operate with His creative intentions, the more fully His action can be seen through us.*

Where men act at their best, there God's action is best revealed. This is why the landmark social legislation begun under Moses in the days of our ancient Jewish ancestors is remembered in the Old Testament as "carved by the Finger of God."

We recognize the Jewish people as inspired by God to be a **vanguard community in mankind's march to history's goal.** In them we find our own beginnings as the *People of God.*** Like our Jewish ancestors, we who are the Church see ourselves as *the community convoked into being by God to be His prophetic finger leading the way through history*.

This prophetic community is called to be the first in every age and every location to stand out in the no-man's land between

---

* Although by modern standards the owning of slaves is a sign of primitive morality, yet by the standards of those days the Old Testament legislation which permitted slavery was quite advanced in its humaneness compared with slavery in pagan lands. The sabbatical year (much like the sabbatical day off each week) was a step forward in human moral evolution.
** Our English word "Church" does not do justice to the reality of what this means. The Jewish word for it is *Qahal*, which means "community convoked into being by God"; the Latin word for it is *ecclesia* (from which we get our word "ecclesiastical") and suggests the same as the Jewish meaning.

54

the No Longer and the Not Yet, serving as God's Finger to point the way, to reform social institutions, and to heal the personal dignity of man.

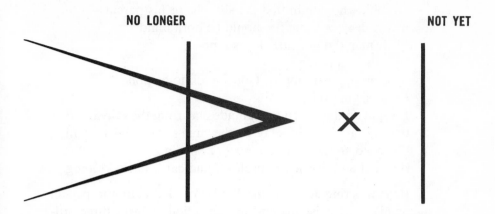

NO LONGER
NOT YET

We the People of God are called to be the vanguard community whose prophetic sensitivity to God's breath in the winds of history makes us alive to evolution in humanness anywhere, and impels us to share it with all men. We see ourselves as a *catholic community* among human communities: a community which cuts across all national or local boundaries, representing not this or that limited human interest but representing *humanness itself*. To be "catholic" is to be "universal"—to embrace and include all, acknowledging neither race nor color nor social class nor geographical boundary as an ultimate distinction between man and man.

The Finger of God incarnate in Jesus. *As Christians, we can interpret the* **Incarnation** *of God in the man Jesus as making Him the high point in evolution, the summit and source of all that man is called by God to become.* For us, He is the Vanguard Man, the first to express in matter the Personality of God, the first human being to have been raised to complete union with God.

Since we have been baptized into His Risen Life, for us **To Live Is Christ.** * *We believe that whatever we do to make the world a better place is an expression of the Christ-life in us.* When we turn our hand to solving the world's problems, we as members of Christ's mystical body extend His personal healing touch to the whole world.

---

* Philippians 1:21.

9:1 Walking along one day,
  Jesus saw a man who was blind since his birth.
  2 His disciples asked him,
    "Rabbi, who committed the sin—he or his parents—
    which deserved that he should be born blind?"
  3 "This man did not sin," Jesus replied,
    "nor did his parents;
    he is an opportunity for God's work to be done." . . .
  6 Upon saying this,
    He spat on the ground and made clay from the saliva;
    then he applied the clay to the man's eyes and told him,
    "Now go and wash in the pool of Siloam" . . .
  7 He went and washed himself off and came back—seeing.

Remembering Jesus as the Finger of God acting in person as our guide, we Christians find in this action of Jesus three attitudes which are necessary for all those who, in His footsteps, wish to put into action a healing concern for the ills of society:

1) Do not blame a person for conditions not of his own making.
2) Get your hands dirty—get involved and *do* something.
3) Respect the needy person's dignity by enabling him to help himself rather than remain dependent.

Three directions for action

All of us are rich in some ways, poor in others. Insofar as we are rich, we have the obligation to share. Insofar as we are poor, we have the opportunity to receive what others have to share with us. Even if and when the human race succeeds in lifting itself as one body out of the gross poverty which has been the condition of some men ever since the hard times of primitive ice ages, there will still be a sense in which "the poor are always with us"—for there will always be the young, who have more to receive from their elders than they can ever repay; there will always be the aged, whose worn bodies can no longer carry the share of the common load which once they could and which now others carry in their stead; there will always be the physically and mentally handicapped, who will need the best of society's extra care and healing powers; there will always be the less talented, who cannot compete with others more brilliant but still need an opportunity to give in a way that fulfills their own capacity; there will always be the selfish, who need the radiance of others' love to convince them that happiness is more in loving than in waiting to be loved; there will always be, in one category or another, persons who need to receive more than they are able to give. But in receiving, they give —for all of us need to give as well as receive; receivers give us the opportunity to give.

Through **justice** (giving others what is their due) and through **charity** (giving others what is their need) we make ourselves part of that which is larger than ourselves—that continuing evolution of the universe toward becoming what it wants to be —the developing human community.

Although there are many kinds of need in the world, we are focusing our attention in this booklet upon the economic side of life, and therefore let us focus our attention upon those needs which arise out of economic poverty in today's world of the runaway explosions described in chapter 2. *In our time, the alleviation of economic poverty and the "poverty culture" often associated with it requires three forms of action:*

I. Direct aid for immediate economic needs:

a) *on the person-to-person level.* In everyone's personal life there are always occasions and opportunities for personal acts of giving or helping. They include such things as serving as a nurses' aid in a hospital, giving money to a blind pencil salesman, collecting Christmas baskets for poor families, giving advice about job opportunities, and countless other personal responses to situations of need among people one knows as individuals.

b) *on the institutional level.* In today's complex world, there are too many people in too many complicated situations for person-to-person help to be sufficient. If someone asks a friend for advice about getting a job, for example, the friend may not know enough about his city to have all the information he needs; or if a whole family of farm workers have been laid off by automation, and all their relatives have previously fallen upon hard times and moved to the city where they are just barely making ends meet, there may be no relatives to whom they can turn for temporary aid while they are relocating themselves. In these and countless other cases, the burden of helping cannot be laid upon the first stranger who happens to come along in the needy person or family's life; society has found it more manageable to bear the neighbor's burden through specialized agencies and institutions, supported by public donations or public tax funds.

This institutionalized aid is required not only on the local scene but internationally as well; it includes foreign aid programs in the form of grants and loans of food, money, technological and agricultural assistance programs, or whatever is immediately needed.

Institutional aid, whether in the form of a local "welfare" agency, or in the form of an international gift or loan program, has two major "bugs" in it at the present time:

1. There are some people who take advantage of these agencies either by fabricating "needs" which do not exist, or by becoming permanently dependent upon the agency rather than seeking for means of self-help.

2. In order to "crack down" on such abuses, the agencies develop a multitude of impersonal regulations which have the unfortunate by-effect of disqualifying many people whose needs are genuine.

The fact that these "bugs" exist in institutional forms of aid to the poor is not an excuse for disparaging the whole idea of public welfare agencies, for they are the only means society has at present for dealing with large-scale socio-economic problems which are simply too overwhelming to be met only on an individual person-to-person basis. But the existence of these hangups calls for constant efforts to improve the methods of the institutions. And more importantly, it calls for efforts to *remove the social problems which cause the needs in the first place*.

II. Changing social structures. Merely giving aid to meet immediate needs is not enough. It is necessary as a stopgap measure, but it does not exhaust our responsibility.

The Christmas basket may be an occasion for sin. It can be simply a conscience-soother to persuade the well-to-do donor that he has done his duty, and it can also jar loose the hopelessness of those who are trapped in need. The Christmas basket can be and often is a means by which the donor enhances his own sense of power and the recipient is made to feel more powerless. You ask, "What do you want me to do? Should I stop giving Christmas baskets?" I answer that there are certainly times and places where giving money and food outright is requisite. Emergencies and personal crises still make this kind of help necessary.

Yet the man who would practice true Christian charity ought to try to find out why the Christmas basket is necessary in this day and age. He must acquaint himself with the facts of the situation, and then devote some of his time and effort to working in some area that needs improvement—for instance, political reform, tutorial programs, interracial and intercultural planning. In any case, he who would give must strive to be a power-sharer; that is, to raise the power level of those who receive. For the receivers of Christmas baskets are no less human beings than the givers.*

Changing social structures includes, on the local scene, such things as: extending minimum-wage legislation; lobbying for workingmen's compensation-for-injury clauses in union contracts; establishing an industry-wide voluntary code for pacing automation in such a way that workingmen will not be replaced by machines until they can be retrained for a new job or relocated in their old job at some other plant (even moving the family to the new location at company expense)—so that their families will not be in a position to need Christmas baskets or welfare checks.

On the international scene, it includes such things as establishing trade policies which contribute to world prosperity, not simply the prosperity of a single nation at the expense of others; working through the United Nations and other international organizations to promote peace and international justice and resist aggressions and injustices, and to help underdeveloped nations establish educational systems and industrial complexes.

III. Education. The first two steps cannot eradicate the worst forms of poverty unless people are educated to make use of the resources available and/or offered to them. Besides the obvious matter of improving the schools which serve the young in areas of poverty, *education is needed for the adult community as well.* Those who are in a position to help need to be educated to the needs of others; especially they need to be educated out of prejudices and into attitudes of creative expectation.**

---

* Alan J. Eichenberger, "Christmas Baskets and Power," *Christian Century*, December 21, 1966, p. 1567.
** See chapter 5, pp. 68-69 for further elaboration of this point.

On the local level, adult education includes educating the poor as to what their legal rights are; training the young and retraining the old for new job opportunities; educating business leaders and politicians to the realities of poverty in the city and around the country; educating prejudiced people to the facts about themselves and other groups; etc.

On the international level, this includes activities such as those sponsored by the Peace Corps and similar Church-related groups; objective and even prophetic news reporting; developing the potential of the mass communications media to be instruments of education, not escape or triviality; etc.

Through the three forms of social action described above, we Christians become The Finger of God in human society, extending to the world the healing touch of Jesus who lives in us. As members of the same Body, when one member hurts we all feel the pain; when one member lacks something, we all feel the loss.

We extend this healing concern not only to those who are Roman Catholics, but to all men—for we believe that all men are united in a common destiny even though they do not have the gift of our Christian faith to fully appreciate what their destiny is.

The mind of Christ

We Christians believe that in the Christ-community, God makes it possible for us to become as human as possible—to be members of the Man who is God-in-matter, making all of the material universe an expression of God's personality in his creation.

The Church's task is to keep earthly things from being gods and thereby enable them to serve man in his attempt to express Godlikeness.

Christian thinking on the economic side of life is an attempt to embody in our lives the thinking which Jesus embodied in His own. Let us look separately at His thinking about *things* and then His thinking about *persons*.

The Value of Things

Rich and poor are relative terms. The ordinary man today is better off than the kings of former ages. Many people who are poor by today's standards would have been considered comfortably rich in other ages. Those who are rich today will be considered primitive in a generation or two. And everybody who is considered rich by other people sees himself as missing out on what those he considers richer than himself have.

There is no human being who does not feel limited and frustrated by his limitations. Everyone wishes his possibilities were greater. The rich and poor are alike in their basic experience of this human condition. In human dignity and worthwhileness of life, the poor person is the equal of the rich man. It all depends on how each lives up to his own possibility.

When Jesus appeared in the world. He did not become a great inventor like Thomas Edison, nor did He become a great political leader like George Washington. He did not frown upon these human achievements; but He saw His role as different; He gave Himself to mankind as the Model and Source of the spiritual dimension of life—the *total living up to life within its limits*. He left the enlarging of material possibility to other men; for Himself He chose the role of illuminating the spiritual possibility *within* mankind's material possibility.

A proper attitude toward material things combines *detachment* and *attachment*.

I. **Detachment.**

Jesus told His followers,

Matthew

5:3 The really happy people in life
are those who are inwardly free from possessions,
for the kingdom of heaven is theirs.

a) **Money** *is not wealth but a means to wealth.* Wealth is the substance of this world's goods. Money is not that substance, but only a medium of exchange for trading substances. It also translates intangible things like time or labor or talent into an equivalent material substance. Money therefore is an abstraction. It is a sign of wealth, a means to wealth, but is not wealth itself.

Therefore it is a matter of common sense not to be more attached to money than to what it can buy. This fault is known as *miserliness*. Persons who hoard money rather than use it for their legitimate needs and the legitimate needs of their dependents, or who sacrifice their happiness for the constantly snowballing preoccupation of piling up more and more money with which to make more and more money, are persons with a deep-seated character flaw of insecurity. They want security at the price of human happiness. They want more security than is possible for human beings. They want protection from being limited. Unfortunately the price they pay for this protection is that they are also "protecting" themselves from the good things of life. They are their own jailers. Rather than enjoy the substance of good things and good company, they wrap themselves up in dollar bags, relishing the promise money holds out but never cashing in on it.

b) **Wealth** *is not humanness but a means to humanness.* Just as money is not identical with wealth, so wealth is not identical with human happiness. Happiness is the sense of fulfillment of one's reason for existing. Wealth is not fulfilment, but is a servant. It is a means of happiness, an expression of humanness, but is not human happiness itself.

Therefore it is a matter of common sense not to be more attached to wealth than to what it can express. This fault is known as *superfluousness*. Persons who conspicuously display their wealth, or luxuriously wallow in it rather than use it for their legitimate needs and the legitimate needs of their dependents and their less wealthy fellow man, or who sacrifice the meaning of life for a mere search after more and more comfort, are persons with a deep-seated character flaw of selfishness. They want pleasure or comfort instead of beauty and sharing love. They want more coming to them than is possible for human beings. They do not know that "it is more blessed to give than to receive" (*Acts* 20:35). They want protection from being productive. Ultimately, the price they pay for this protection is that they are also "protecting" themselves from the conviction that they are worthwhile. Rather than enjoy life by creating and sharing, they try to absorb life like passive sponges, relishing the suds but not the substance of life.

II. Attachment

Not one to disdain material things, Jesus made water become wine at the wedding of Cana; yet He did not make stones become bread in the desert. He praised the widow who gave everything including her last 2¢ to the Temple treasury; yet He did not tell Mary of Bethany to sell her expensive ointment for alms to give the poor, but He accepted her lavishing it upon Himself as an expression of her love.

He was sensitive to the inner meaning of things, and that meaning was: persons. When *things* express *man's love for man,* things are man's friend; when things express man's runaway tendencies for meaningless pleasure or isolated splendor, they are man's master and make him a slave.

Like Jesus Christ, the Church has the task in history of showing men how to be human. Like Jesus, she does not condemn

63

money or wealth, nor does she require that everybody be reduced to as common a level of poverty as possible. She blesses the material progress of civilization and tries to make it available to mankind, but always with the spiritual dimension and meaning paramount. In the spirit of Christ, she encourages man to use his economic and technological efforts to turn the "water" of natural resources into the "wine" of good things for all of mankind to celebrate.

Hence, men should have a positive, creative, respectful attitude toward material things. We should endeavor to cultivate the practical arts and the fine arts. This implies conservation of natural resources; artistic rather than ugly design in architecture and city planning; receptiveness toward beauty wherever it is found—whether in ancient, classical, or modern art and music and sculpture and dance; and being *alive* to a sense of music in the noises of everyday life, a sense of beauty in the scenes of daily existence, a feeling for the essence of things we contact, and a keenness to the rhythm of life's beat.

Prejudice of Persons

James

> 2:1 My brothers,
> don't try to pick and choose among people
> along with faith in Jesus Christ the Lord of Glory.
> 2 For example, suppose a man comes into your assembly
> wearing an upper-class suit and a gold ring,
> and along with him comes in a poor man
> in shabby clothes—
> 3 and you take a look at the well-dressed man
> and say, "You take the good seat over here,"
> but you tell the poor man,
> "Look, you stand over there" or
> "You can sit on the floor by my footstool."
> 4 Aren't you sitting in judgment over one another
> and passing rash judgments at that?
> 8 But if you keep the basic law of Scripture,

"You shall love your neighbor as yourself,"
then you will do the right thing.
⁹ However, if you act like snobs,
you are sinning against this law.

By the very nature of social living, we are constantly dividing other people into two classes: an *in-group* and an *out-group*. The in-group consists of everybody who is "in" with me, every group I feel I take some part in; the out-group consists of all the outsiders.

We usually surround ourselves with several in-groups, one inside the other like concentric circles. For example, my family is one in-group; a wider in-group is my circle of friends; my school is another; my city, my country, my religious denomination are others. Every one of these in-groups has its corresponding out-group: some other family, another crowd, a different school, another city, foreign countries, members of another religion.

In-groups and out-groups are a normal part of human life. However, they can often be distorted into something abnormal. This happens when they are created for selfish reasons, or when a legitimate distinction is exaggerated. For example, one's family is an in-group and certain considerations should be given to members of one's family as compared with outsiders; yet, "family snobbery" should be avoided. Again, members of one's own religious group share an interpretation of life which others do not completely share; yet this should not be an excuse for feeling personally superior to members of other religions or for excluding them from one's friendship or from sharing other aspects of life which one may have in common with them.

One of the most common and damaging forms of exaggerated group-consciousness is group **prejudice.**

Prejudice—what is it? Who has it?

Prejudice (from Latin *pre-judicium*) means pre-judgment. It means forming a judgment before all the evidence is in.

In the early summer season two Toronto newspapers carried between them holiday advertisements from approximately 100 different resorts. A Canadian social scientist, S. L. Wax, undertook an interesting experiment. To each of these hotels and resorts he wrote two letters, mailing them at the same time, and asking for room reservations for exactly the same dates. One letter he signed with the name "Mr. Greenberg," the other with the name "Mr. Lockwood." Here are the results:

To "Mr. Greenberg":

52 per cent of the resorts replied;

36 per cent offered him accomodations.

To "Mr. Lockwood":

95 per cent of the resorts replied;

93 per cent offered him accomodations.

Thus, nearly all of the resorts in question welcomed Mr. Lockwood as a correspondent and as a guest; but nearly half of them failed to give Mr. Greenberg the courtesy of a reply, and only slightly more than a third were willing to receive him as a guest.

None of the hotels knew "Mr. Lockwood" or "Mr. Greenberg." For all they knew "Mr. Greenberg" might be a quiet, orderly gentleman, and "Mr. Lockwood" rowdy and drunk. The decision was obviously made not on the merits of the individual, but on "Mr. Greenberg's" supposed membership in a group.*

We can be prejudiced *for* something or *against* it. We can be prejudiced for or against *things, persons,* or *groups.*

Prejudice *for* something or someone cannot exist unless there also exists along with it a prejudice *against* the opposite. For example, I might like strawberry ice cream; but I could hardly be said to be "prejudiced" in favor of strawberry ice cream unless I am aware that other flavors exist but don't give them a chance. Or, I might like my friends; but I would not be "prejudiced" in favor of my friends unless there were some other people in one way or another opposed to my friends, and I agreed with my friends or favored them without actually considering the merits of the case.

Why do we judge a thing, or a person, or a group, before we have seen all the evidence? Here are some of the reasons which contribute to prejudice:

1. *Mental laziness.* Life is so much simpler if we go around with a few general statements that apply to all cases; that way we don't have to make the effort of constantly studying each new situation, each new person. Often this involves creating a **stereotype** —a mental picture of the "typical" member of a group which

---

* Gordon Allport, *The Nature of Prejudice* (Garden City: Doubleday Anchor Book, 1958), p. 5.

emphasizes positive qualities if the group is "my" group or negative qualities if it is the "other" group.

2. *Unexamined education.* Many times we pick up our prejudices from the society around us, including at times even our parents and teachers. We hear adults making oversimplified statements about current events or particular groups, and we take their judgments as our own without studying the complicated issues for ourselves.

3. *Misinformation concerning facts.* Sometimes, even when we do go out of our way to get the facts on an issue, we gather our facts from unreliable sources—rumor, partisan propaganda, etc. Or if we go to more reliable sources, we try to obtain only those facts we want to hear and neglect to remember or pay attention to facts on the other side of the case.

4. *Advantage.* We have an unconscious feeling that, if we look at the facts objectively, we might not get our way as much as we can if we make up our own facts in advance, or carefully filter the facts until we see only what we want to see. We generally tend to be prejudiced in favor of ourselves and against whatever or whoever seems to limit or oppose us. This natural prejudice toward ourselves usually includes our in-group considered as an extension of ourselves, against whoever is the corresponding out-group.

5. *Escalation of hostility.* Sometimes, where in-groups and out-groups exist, a wall of fear and suspicion grows between them. If fear reaches a certain point, they become afraid to communicate with each other. Once this happens, fear of the known grows into that monster which is fear of the unknown. Then both sides confuse their own imaginations about one another for real facts.

6. *Pride.* We all have a tendency to reassure ourselves that we are good by convincing ourselves we are better than someone else. From here it is an easy step to keep before our minds some out-group or individual that we can keep telling ourselves is worse than ourselves and our group. If we hear anything bad about such a person or group we say, "See—that confirms the low opinion I have of them." If we hear anything good about the same person or group we say, "It probably isn't true," or "That's just the exception that proves the rule."

7. *Negative expectation.* In situations of mutual hostility, persons or groups sometimes find themselves in a vicious circle. A mixture of facts, partial facts, and untruths combine to give both sides a prejudice concerning the future—a conviction that

mutual relationships can never get any better but can only get worse. Because each person or group knows the other side also feels that way, this negative expectation becomes a *self-fulfilling prophecy*. Neither person or group is willing to give the other a chance because each is convinced the other will not give oneself a chance.

If we wish to become aware of our own prejudices and correct them, we need to cultivate the opposites to the seven factors listed above:

1. *Mental alertness.* We ought to be constantly testing our general statements, never applying them automatically to every member of a group, but seeing to it that each person or situation is judged on their unique merits.

2. *Critical examination of one's own background.* We should never allow the persons we consider authorities in our lives to do all of our thinking for us—especially the nebulous "authority" of "Everybody knows . . ." or "They say . . ." When others make general statements about other persons or groups we should make them produce facts.

3. *Search for the facts.* We should try to get *all* the facts on both sides of an issue, and obtain them from the most reliable sources.

4. *Golden Rule.* Rather than seek our own advantage in a selected interpretation of carefully filtered facts, we should treat every neighbor as ourselves and try to find as many facts favorable to his or their side of an issue as we can for ours. This does not mean trying to become prejudiced in reverse, for someone else against ourselves or our groups. It means making sure we have the whole truth by *looking* for *all* the facts whether they contribute to our own case or not.

5. *Communication.* Where fears and animosities exist between individuals and groups, the only remedy against runaway imaginations is keeping the channels of communication open between the persons and groups.

6. *Humility.* We need to give up the illusion that we have to be better than somebody else or some other group. Then we will be able to see that our own faults are as bad (or worse) as others'. Then we are free to begin working together to improve matters on both sides of the fence.

7. *Creative expectation.* We all know how we feel when someone has a negative attitude against us. We feel we haven't got

a chance. We feel defeated before we start; we feel that any good we do will be suspect or unnoticed. We feel that any bad we do will be exaggerated; anything we do which is ambiguous or mistaken will be interpreted as certainly evil and ill-intentioned. We become self-conscious and, in spite of ourselves, make blunders.

On the other hand, when we know we are regarded with a positive attitude, we can taste success even when just beginning. We know that our good efforts will be well received, and that our mistakes will be seen as well-intentioned rather than ill-intentioned. We are encouraged to make better efforts, our ideals are strengthened, and we have a loyalty to those who love us, which brings out the best in us.

It is the same way with other people and other groups. We can trap them in our own poor image of them, or we can open to them a world of possibility by our creative attitude toward their own possibilities. Rather than communicating that we have something against them, we communicate that *they have something for us—something to give, something to be proud of.*

Prejudice hinders human progress, both in the prejudiced person or group, and in the person or group against whom the prejudice is directed. For progress in society is impossible without co-operation. But creative expectation makes it possible for progress to happen.

The Lord's Supper

As we saw on pp. 5-11, human society has become civilized through the developments of progress in three interconnected sides of life: economic, political, and cultural. And as we saw on pp. 61-69, we who are the Church see ourselves as a prophetic community called into being by God to point the way, to reform, to heal society's ills. While the whole world consists of "God's people," there exists among them *The People of God* who are called to be the Christ-community putting the Mind of Christ into action in the world.

In this booklet we have briefly sketched the Christ-community's sense of responsibility toward the economic aspect of civilization's progress into trans-civilization. But economic progress alone is not enough to ensure a meaningful life. There must be a cultural *vision of life* to give a sense of direction to man's efforts to improve the lot of man.

This vision of life needs to be celebrated in some way. *The Christ-community has a cultural vision of life which it celebrates in the form of* **worship.** In this chapter we will see how our worship helps us celebrate man's march through time toward the end of history.

Celebrating salvation history

Old Testament symbol. In the history of the Jewish people's founding under Moses, we find the symbol of man's march through time.

12:31 Pharaoh called Moses and Aaron in the dead of night
and said, "Go—leave my people,
you and the Israelites!" . . .

34 So the people took bread before it was leavened,
and, wrapping it in their cloaks,
they carried it over their shoulders.

37 And the Israelites started out from Rameses . . .

39 And they baked the dough
which only a short while ago
they had brought out of Egypt;
and they made unleavened biscuits,
for there had been no time to leaven it,
with the Egyptians hurrying them away . . .

13:3 And Moses spoke to the people:
"This day on which you came out of Egypt,
out of slavery—
remember it and eat unleavened bread—
for Yahweh has brought you here with a Mighty hand!"

16:1 . . . Now on the fifteenth day of the second month
after their departure from Egypt,

2 the whole community of Israelites complained
against Moses and Aaron in the desert . . .

3 "If only we could have lived in Egypt
until Yahweh ended our days!
Those were the days
when we sat over pots of meat and ate our fill of bread.
Why have you brought us out here in the desert?
To kill the whole lot of us with starvation?"

4 But Yahweh said to Moses,
"Behold, I will send down bread from heaven for you.
Let the people go out each day
and gather what they need . . ."

13 And in the morning a dew lay round about their camp,

14 all over the ground, looking like frost on the desert.

31 The Israelites called it manna;
it was like a white grain and tasted like honey-bread.

35 The Israelites ate this manna for forty years
until they came to fertile land;
they were fed with it until they reached the borders
of the Land of Canaan.

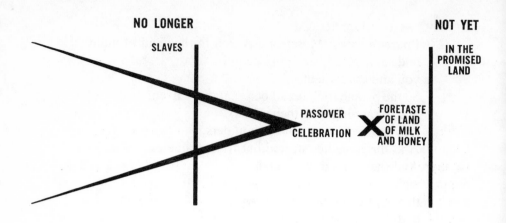

No longer slaves to their past, *not yet* in the Promised Land of the future, the People of God journey through the sands of time celebrating God's victory over the past but not yet seeing its fulfillment; they are nourished on hope, on a foretaste of the Land of Milk and Honey that is not yet visible.

2. **New Testament sacrament.** When Jesus founded His community to be the fulfillment of what God had started through Moses, he combined these two symbolic celebrations in one at the Lord's Supper:

Luke

22:14 When the hour had come,
 He sat down to eat with His twelve apostles.
 15 He told them, "I have been greatly looking forward
 to eat this Passover meal with you before I suffer;
 16 for I tell you, I will not eat it again
 until it is fulfilled in the Kingdom of God."
 18 Taking bread, He gave thanks
 and divided it to give them, saying,
 "This is My Body, which is given for you.
 Do this in memory of Me."

John

6:48 "I am the Bread of life.
 49 Your ancestors ate manna in the desert
 and they are dead.
 50 But this is the Bread coming down from heaven
 —if you eat of it you will not die.

72

51 I am the Living Bread
which has come down from heaven.
58 . . . As I live because of The Father,
so he who eats of me will live because of Me."

We Christians believe that by being baptized into Jesus Christ we become sharers of the Risen Life which is His. We, the Christ-community, see ourselves as the New People of God, journeying through the sands of time. When we partake of the Lord's Supper, we celebrate our belief that we are *no longer* slaves to mortal human life; we also receive it as the Bread of Heaven sustaining us while we do *not yet* see our own Risen Life fulfilled.

We look forward to the Celebration at the end of time when the Kingdom of God is made manifest: when the Living Christ-in-community has completely refashioned the human community so that it radiates in an obvious way the fact that it is His Mystical Body. Another poetic image (for how else can such things be described?) for the destiny of the developing human community is given in the final book of our Bible, the Apocalypse (attributed to St. John the apostle):

Apocalypse

19:6 I heard a voice
roaring like a crowd or like a waterfall
or like thunder, proclaiming:
"Alleluia! The Lord our God almighty resigns!
7 Let us be glad and celebrate in His honor—
for the marriage of the Lamb has come,
and His Bride has prepared herself!"
21:1 And I saw a new heaven and a new earth! . . .
2 And I, John, saw the holy city
New Jerusalem
coming down from heaven from God,
dressed like a bride adorned for her Spouse.
3 And I heard a mighty voice ring out from the throne:
"Here is God's tent among men,
and He will pitch His tent among them,
They shall be His People,
and God-with-them shall be their God.
4 And God will wipe every tear from their eyes,
and no longer will there be death

or groaning or crying or sorrow,
for all these things have vanished!
⁵ "Behold," said the One on the throne,
"I am making all things New!"

Whenever Christians gather to celebrate The Lord's Supper, we celebrate that we are *no longer* mere men, slaves to death and suffering and the inflicting of suffering on our fellow men; we celebrate and make present symbolically that which we already are but which is *not yet* fulfilled: we are the community which is God's presence in the world making all things new so that at the end of time what is now apparent only in symbol and faith will be apparent to the eyes.

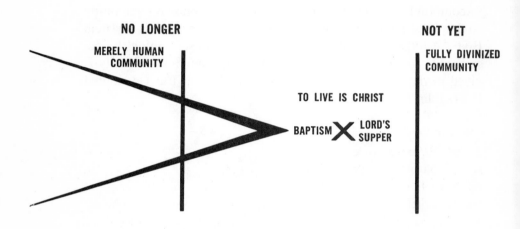

The Parish: a community of history makers

In mankind's march through the sands of time, history is not something that just "happens" to men; *history is something that men make happen!*

The Christian vision of life is one in which *God makes history happen by working through the actions of men.* History is not a journey from nowhere to nowhere; it is not a meaningless cycle of repetitions; it is a pilgrimage from unfulfillment to fulfillment. History is man's part in the New Creation. When men make history they are co-operating with God in the making of the universe, bringing it to finished perfection.

When we Christians gather to celebrate The Lord's Supper, we are celebrating our belief that we are history makers. The Mass is a dinner at which Revolutionaries gather in the presence of their Leader to celebrate what has been accomplished and to commit themselves to the completion of what has been begun.

The Christian revolution is to develop the human community into the Body of Christ. The revolution begins first among Christians; we pledge to be the vanguard in removing from our own ranks all that belongs to the *No Longer*—we pledge to be the first to remove poverty from the world, to remove all forms of unfreedom or unfair advantage over one's fellow man, the first to remove ignorance and spread the light of a meaningful life to all men.

The Christian revolution is not fought with guns or destructive actions; it is fought with love and constructive action. The parish is meant to be an avant-garde center of social progress. It is not meant to be a refuge from the burning issues of the day, but it is meant to be the headquarters where Divine Love celebrates its successes and plots its next moves.

Today, when our American cities are undergoing such drastic changes and growth pains, the obligation of Christian worship-communities is clear. Those who gather to pray together on Sunday are being convoked to be the Christ-community: to lay the healing Finger of God upon the needs of their fellow man.

Each city parish is called to be a center where Christians take their neighborhood and their entire metropolitan area seriously and study its immediate and long-range needs in view of the monumental changes affecting the cities. Such problems as poverty, the welfare system, integration, the improvement of the schools, and so on, are city-wide problems. Each parish needs to ask how it can utilize its own people and resources to help develop the human community of which they are a part.

In our time, the prayer-life and worship-life of Christians is being called to develop a modern style—one which is both active and meditative. It is called to be *active* in the sense that prayer and worship should not become a refuge or escape from involvement in the needs of humanity; rather, union with God should unite us with His action in the world. On the other hand, there is a need for a good deal of *meditative reflection*. There are many active revolutionaries in the world today whose methods are destructive, because their goals are not properly thought out—they seek retaliation rather than justice. Hence the Christian worship-community should be a place where action is judged in the light of prayerful love for the world. Personal union with God is the only way to assure that our social actions will develop a really God-like community.

Your parish is or will be going through its own growth pains as more and more Christians come to understand what they are doing when they come to Church. Continuing experiments with the style of common worship will be attempting to help you celebrate more consciously what it means to be the People of God in today's history-making times. Continuing development of new study and action projects, with closer involvement of priests, religious, and lay people will be attempting to offer you an outlet for your constructive services in developing the human community according to the Mind of Christ.

Meaningful Christian life is the antidote to a large-scale movement in our times: the growing number of **history drop-outs.** These are individuals or groups (many of them your own age) who are fed up with the *No Longer* but are not giving themselves to any constructive efforts to work toward the *Not Yet.* They react against the poverty, injustice, and prejudice which they see in the world around them by just "pulling out." Instead of really knowing how to celebrate, they get meaningless "kicks" through using alcohol, sex, or other forms of escape addiction. Some seek to *find* love in isolated adolescent communities rather than to *give* love where the needs of their fellow man in the larger world exist.

When you leave high school and enter career life or college life or armed services life, you will have to make some basic personal decisions about where you stand on the burning issues connected with society's growing pains. You will have to decide whether to be a history-maker or a history drop-out.

You can drop out of history in two ways: 1) by rejecting society and its problems and going your own individualistic or escape-community's way; or 2) by not even bothering to reject society but being caught up in it without thinking, being a defender of the status quo.

On the other hand, you can be a history-maker in two ways: 1) by engaging in economic, political, or cultural action which is helpful to others in society but without having any sense of ulti-mate vision of what it's all for; or 2) by engaging in economic, political, or cultural action *because* you are a Christian making Christ ever more present in the world. If you choose this latter alternative, you will be accepting the responsibility of helping your parish or college or armed services worship-community be-come a real, living, dynamic force in the world. The Bishops of Vatican Council II have only begun the process of bringing the Church up to date; *your* generation of laymen, religious, priests and bishops coming from *your* ranks will be the ones who make or break the reform.

FOCUS

ORLANDO CABANBAN

The Negro exodus

The development of the human community will be man's task as long as history lasts. This development takes place on many fronts at every moment. However, in each age of history there are a few tasks which are the "cutting edge" of progress. Solve the problems connected with these focal tasks, and the problems connected with related tasks will fall in line, giving little resistance.

The problem of poverty, hunger, and lack of awareness of one's own unique gifts is a world-wide problem; its focus is the slums of large cities; in these cities there are many groups who experience the complicated tangle of economic, political, and cultural deprivation which we call "poverty"; but *in our American cities the focal group in whom all these realities are brought to a head is the Negro community*. Not all Negroes are poor or live in slums; and not all poor people and slum-dwellers are Negro. But the majority of Negroes live in slums and the majority of slum-dwellers in our large American cities are Negroes. Whatever problems are connected with poverty must be solved among this group as the "cutting edge" of the solution of poverty in America (and from there outward to the world).

In mankind's pilgrimage, from the injustice, slavery, inequality, and prejudice which can *no longer* be tolerated, to the golden age of brotherhood which is *not yet* achieved, the most notable group of pilgrims making this Exodus from slavery to the Promised Land in our country are the American Negroes. No longer slaves in the strict sense of the word, they are not yet full partners in our nation's economic abundance, not yet treated as first-class citizens in its political life, not yet able to give and receive their brotherly share of the nation's cultural life.

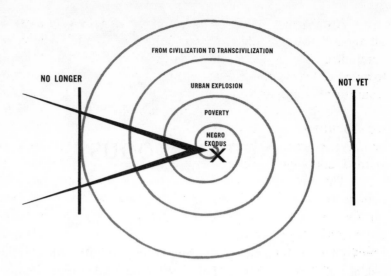

But the American dream, and the future of world transcivilization, require that we all make it together. If the developing human community gets "hung up" at the stage of racial integration, it cannot go forward in other stages of the not yet completed task of making one world, one family of God.

Because the Negro entrance into our promised land is the most pressing nation-wide need of American social development in our time, every Christian needs to be knowledgeable about the Negro's problems, even if there is not yet a large Negro population in his own area. If the problems of your local situation concern another minority group, the following articles might still be of some profit by comparing the readings to your own situation to see where there are similarities and differences.

The advance in Negro self-recognition is complicated by two factors which have caused and intensified the poverty experience among these people: 1) a history of slavery and its by-effects; 2) an easily distinguishable physical characteristic which, unlike a foreign language, cannot be changed and stands as a permanent target for prejudice.

As the Church, the vanguard community among human communities, we believe it is our job to point the way for humanity's advance in brotherhood. The Good News of Christ has been translated into a statement of principles in this area on behalf of the Catholic Church by the body of American Catholic Bishops in their classic statement of 1958. (Cf. pp. 100-105.)

An abstract statement of principles is relatively easy. We all agree that we should "love our fellow man." We all agree that "prejudice" is bad. We all agree that we should go out of our way to help our fellow man rise above his problems when he needs and wants our help to do so.

But there is much room for honest disagreement as to *how* we should love our fellow man, *when* our attitude is prejudiced or only realistic, *how much co-operation* is really possible and wanted, and *what methods* are constructive or destructive.

These issues are being debated today in thought, word, and action. You can keep abreast of them by following current events on TV, in the newspapers and magazines, as well as in various movie and stage presentations. Space does not allow us to go into detail on all the problems connected with the American Negro's exodus from poverty to plenty. But we include in the pages that follow a sampling of articles discussing *one* of the problems—that of housing. In reading these various articles, you may want to have a red pen handy, marking items as "economic, political, or cultural"; or as "cause" and "effect"; or as "fact" and "prejudice"; or by writing comments and questions in the margin.

Problems

Confessions of a Block-Buster*

A Chicago real-estate agent who moves Negro families into all-white blocks reveals how he reaps enormous profits from racial prejudice.

> In this article you will be wanting to look for the answer to such questions as:
>
> 1. How do some people make the problems of house-finding more complicated than they have to be?
>
> 2. Why are some white home-owners afraid of having Negroes move into their block?
>
> 3. How is the practice of "blockbusting" unfair to persons who live in a neighborhood?
>
> 4. How is it unfair to those who wish to move to a neighborhood?
>
> 5. How can real estate policies ease or increase the city's growing pains?
>
> 6. What other factors besides real estate policies influence whether or not racial integration will be harmful or beneficial to the old and new residents of a neighborhood?

* By Norris Vitchek as told to Alfred Balk; reprinted from *Saturday Evening Post*, July 14, 1962, pp. 15-19.

Not long ago in an all-white block on Chicago's West Side, a FOR SALE sign appeared in front of a modest frame bungalow. Immediately a wave of fear swept across the block. A Negro family already was living several blocks away. Not far beyond that was the western edge of Chicago's "Black Belt." Every year its border had been moving closer, enclosing blocks like the one along the way. Suppose the bungalow came into possession of a Negro? What would happen to the rest of the block? . . .

"Relax," said the bungalow owner. "I'm selling this through a white real estate man. I won't even talk to a Negro."

Imagine their shock, then, when the FOR SALE sign came down and the new owners moved in—Negroes. And consider the impact of what happened next. Three more buildings, which were already owned by property speculators, "turned" immediately. Other Negro families arrived to look at homes in the block. . . .

Almost overnight a family with four children sold out at a considerable loss. So did six other homeowners in quick succession. "We'll stay," a few owners said. "We're broad-minded." But the situation was out of their control. Finally the last of the whites left —whether or not they could afford to move. Like hundreds of others who have been similarly blitzed, they never really knew what had hit them.

I knew. I triggered the whole sequence of events by buying the bungalow and quickly selling it to a Negro. I am a block-buster . . .

I specialize in locating blocks which I consider ripe for racial change. Then I "bust" them by buying properties from the white owners and selling them to Negroes—with the intent of breaking down the rest of the block for colored occupancy. . . .

I make my money—quite a lot of it, incidentally—in three ways: (1) By beating down the prices I pay the white owners by stimulating their fear of what is to come; (2) by selling the eager Negroes at inflated prices; (3) by financing these purchases at what amounts to a very high rate of interest. . . .

If you are an average white citizen, with average prejudices, you may regard all this as the ruin of metropolitan neighborhoods. I think of it merely as more business. . . . My attitude stems from the fact that few white neighborhoods welcome Negroes who can afford to buy there. . . . My function . . . is to drive the whites from a block whether or not they want to go, then move in Negroes. . . .

So it went in my typical South Side block. . . . We speculators and brokers, both white and Negro, went to work. One paid several Negroes with noisy cars to begin driving up and down the street a few times a day. He also paid a Negro mother who drew aid-to-dependent children payments to walk the block regularly with her youngsters. Another arranged to have phone calls made in the block for such people as "Johnnie Mae." Sometimes calls would consist only of a whisper, a drunken laugh or a warning— such as, "They're coming!" . . .

I began my work in this case by sending a postcard to everyone in the block and others in adjacent blocks. The cards said, "I will pay cash for your building." That was all except for my phone number. The word "cash" was the key. It assured homeowners they could get out quickly and reminded them that their neighbors could too. Then a canvasser and I headed for the block to repeat the offer in person.

No matter how emotional or awkward some situations may be, there is one compensation for it all—money. Some brokers or investors make a good return only on some deals. I make it on every deal in the three ways I mentioned earlier.

You may believe your home is worth $15,000, for example. If I bust your block, I will expect to buy it for $12,000 cash. The odds are that eventually you will sell for that price, if not to me, then to another speculator. If you and your white neighbors did not run, you probably would gain, rather than lose. More than four fifths of the white neighborhoods into which Negroes move hold their own or enjoy an increase in value, according to a five-year Fund for the Republic study of 10,000 transactions in Northern interracial neighborhoods. But the myth that "Negroes lower property values" persists—so whites run, and we block-busters clean up. Within a few days comes profit No. 2: I advertise and sell it to a Negro not for $15,000, but for $18,000. Financing the deal myself, I will accept $500 to $1500 down, with the remainder on contract. The easy-payment plan, I believe it is called —that is, $150 to $200 a month until the contract is fulfilled. When is that? This is profit No. 3, the big one. The contract is fulfilled when I have been paid principal and interest totalling $36,000.

These terms, I am told, force Negroes to overcrowd and overuse their buildings by renting out part of them, or to skimp on maintenance, starting the neighborhood on the way to blight. (In

86

most Negro neighborhoods in Chicago the population density is five times that of white areas.) The contract burden, I am also told, forces Negro mothers to work, despite the presence of youngsters at home, compels fathers to take two jobs and can lead to numerous other problems because of the financial strain and anxiety.

Even so, the number of Negro buyers who default on their payments is small. When it does happen in my own business . . . I keep all the payments made until that time, evict the owners and either rent the building or resell it on about the same terms. . . .

Why should I feel guily? Am I really the basic cause of whites' fleeing? Do I depress the property values and inflate prices for Negroes? When a Negro has been turned away from a bank, do I "trap" him into accepting a contract sale?

And what alternative can you provide for my function? Would you try to influence your bank or savings-and-loan association to begin lending to Negroes? Would you help remove the pressure on "busted" areas by welcoming a Negro family into your block? Do you even care that my business operates as it does? Whatever my faults and whatever the social stigma I endure, I don't believe I am hypocritical about all this. Can you honestly say the same?

Further questions that might come to mind after reading this article are:

7. Should Negroes move out of slum areas?

8. Do all Negro neighborhoods become slums?

9. Should all the former residents move away when Negroes move into a neighborhood?

10. What does a neighborhood need to do in order for integration to be constructive rather than be an occasion for decline?

11. Are old and new residents helpless at the hands of financial operators?

Negroes and Property Values*

What happens to real-estate values when Negroes move into a previously all-white neighborhood?

> The preceding article described problems which arise when unscrupulous men use other peoples' fears for their own gain. These next two articles describe professional attempts to get at the real facts concerning the economics of integrated neighborhoods.
>
> In reading these two articles you will be wanting to look for the answer to such questions as:
>
> 12. To what extent are peoples' attitudes toward other groups based on real facts?
>
> 13. How easy or difficult is it to really get at the economic facts of an issue as large as integration?
>
> 14. How do peoples' negative or creative expectations influence what is going to happen?
>
> 15. Does integration in housing ever work?

A housewife in an upper middle-class neighborhood was asked her reaction to a Negro family's purchase of a house a few doors away. She had no personal objection to them. "They're a fine family—the father's a surgeon," she said, but added this worry . . .

"People drive by and see their little boy playing on the sidewalk. How are they to know he is a doctor's son?"

The incident illustrates a little-recognized fact: What makes many whites uneasy (or worse) about living in an interracial neighborhood is the fear of losing social status. If Negroes live there as maids, janitors or caretakers, no one creates a fuss. Such workers are not there under conditions implying equality of status, and so they are not seen as a threat to their white neighbors. . . .

The most commonly expressed reason for fighting against residential integration, however, is not the fear of losing status but the fear of losing part of one's property investment. "Negroes depreciate property values". . . .

---

* By Bob Senser; reprinted from *Ave Maria*, Feb. 25, 1961.

But is it true that Negroes do depreciate property values? Until recently, even most authorities could answer that question only by guesswork based on limited experience in older neighborhoods. Years ago Negroes coming to Chicago, Detroit and other Northern cities settled only in the older sections, which already were slums and near-slums.

Not all real-estate spokesmen drew hasty conclusions from this. Belden Morgan, past president of both the Chicago and the Los Angeles chapters of the Society of Residential Appraisers, pointed out: "Blaming Negroes for slums is akin to blaming the prisoners for the existence of . . . concentration camps. . . ." The primary cause of slum conditions, Morgan said, is "the advancing age of the structures coupled with the lack of maintenance by indifferent and greedy absentee owners who knew it was not necessary to maintain the properties to hold tenants when the shortage of housing was so acute."

The property-values issue is so important that a group of leading citizens, known as the Commission on Race and Housing, decided to meet it head-on. They launched a full-scale study of the facts. Among its 17 members the commission numbered six men from mortgage banking institutions and the housing industry. Dr. Luigi Laurenti, housing economist from the University of California, was appointed to direct the study.

How to get at the truth? . . . The obvious source was in real-estate transactions themselves: the prices actually paid for homes.

Which homes? Dr. Laurenti stayed clear of slums and near-slums for this reason . . . : "More often than not, residential areas which non-whites are permitted to enter are older neighborhoods where the housing is already obsolescent or deteriorating. . . ."

So Dr. Laurenti focused his study on single-family residential neighborhoods away from the center of town. He studied neighborhoods in an Eastern city, Philadelphia, and two Western cities, San Francisco and Oakland. . . .

His staff members collected nearly 10,000 real-estate prices in all. They traced price changes over a six-year period in 39 all-white and newly-interracial neighborhoods and made 34 inter-community comparisons.

After analyzing a stack of statistics, graphs and charts, Dr. Laurenti came to this conclusion: The entry of Negroes into a neighborhood *rarely* causes the price of residential property to fall—and quite often causes it to rise.

"Considering all of the evidence," says Dr. Laurenti, "the odds are about four to one that house prices in a neighborhood entered by non-whites will keep up with or exceed prices in a comparable all-white area." . . .

Studies made in Portland, Oregon, Kalamazoo, Michigan, Kansas City, Missouri, and other cities, though not as exhaustive and thorough as Dr. Laurenti's, lend support to this point.

This does not mean, of course, that race makes no difference at all in determining real-estate prices. It often does. But the effect of racial considerations is more complicated than most people realize. No single formula will tell you what happens to prices if a Negro buys in a particular neighborhood; but here is a partial list of factors that can influence prices in such a situation:

1) Will the whites become panic-stricken and sell their property at the first opportunity? The hasty sale of homes—usually not to Negroes but to real-estate speculators—pushes prices down. Speculators in Chicago and other cities have made fabulous profits on such sales.

2) How many whites are willing to buy in the neighborhood? . . .

3) Are other Negroes anxious to buy in the neighborhood? Again, the more people that bid on a home, the better the chance the owner has to get a good price.

4) What is the purchasing power of local Negroes? There won't be many Negro buyers if the home hunters are mainly unskilled laborers or families just recently arrived from the rural South. But the Negro middle class has grown tremendously in recent years.

5) What is the price level of homes elsewhere in the city? . . .

6) Does the community include "white elephant" homes? Old mansions, with (say) 12 rooms, are difficult to sell today even to whites. Their market value has been declining for years.

7) How gradual is the racial change in the neighborhood? A smooth transition diminishes the chances of a sharp decline in values.

8) Do the whites have a bitter hostility toward Negroes? An atmosphere of tension will discourage both Negro and white buyers.

9) Will the city enforce its building code and prohibit landlords from cutting up apartments into overcrowded kitchenettes?

And does the neighborhood have a citizens' organization that will work to keep the area a desirable place to live? . . .

You will note that a great deal depends on the attitudes of white people themselves. Ironically, if they take a pessimistic view of the future of property values they can create the very loss they hope to avert.

Sociologist Robert K. Merton speaks of this as a "self-fulfilling prophecy." If enough people believe that a bank is going to fail, they can start a run on that bank and may cause it to close down, at least temporarily. . . .

Similarly, the belief that Negroes hurt property values will also have an impact on the market. For example, it can cause some whites to sell at prices lower than what they could have received had they not held the belief.

In Deerfield, Illinois, a year ago, many whites argued "property values will fall" as they successfully fought a proposed interracial development in their Chicago suburb. During the public furor, publicized internationally, two builders dropped plans to construct all-white subdivisions, and hence land prices fell. The sales price of homes, already suffering from a sluggish market, dropped further still. This has been cited as evidence of how Negroes affect values—although no Negro had purchased a home there and probably none will in the foreseeable future. Actually, the attitude of the people proved to be a "self-fulfilling prophecy" that injured those who propounded it. . . .

In recent years Negroes have moved into several well-kept communities of single family residences. With higher incomes than their parents, many are pouring their money and energies into improving their homes beyond the level maintained by the former white occupants. . . .

The tragedy is that these communities have become part of the all-Negro ghetto, where few whites can have contact with them. . . . Middle and upper-income Negroes, if allowed to move into more of the all-white outskirts of the city, could give a practical answer to the erroneous belief that Negroes inevitably cause property to deteriorate.

One hopeful sign of the future is a new trend—the integration of some neighborhoods previously all-Negro. Along the lake front on Chicago's near South Side, in an area once solidly Negro, 15 skyscraper apartment buildings have been erected. When the first buildings went up, the residents were almost all Negro. Today

91

the area's 10,000 population is 50 per cent white, 50 per cent Negro.

Property values? The New York Life Insurance Company, which owns 10 of the buildings, considers them a good investment —so much so that it plans to invest more of its money into housing nearby—and this, too, will be interracial.

One real-estate authority, Peter Grimm, points out, "The value of anything, including land and buildings, is subjective." The important subjective element in housing and race is the attitude of whites. The more that they lose their racial fears and prejudices, the less they will have to fear about losses in property values.

Counteracting a Racial Myth*

Will residential values decline when Negroes move into white neighborhoods? Apparently not, according to a study by Sherwood Ross, a Washington, D.C., consultant on racial affairs, who checked the U.S. census-listed values of 1,329,762 homes in 47 major cities listed in 1,810 census tracts. He found that in the 1950-60 period the median value of homes in 1,793 of the tracts increased, those in 15 declined, those in one remained the same. Losses averaged no more than 5 percent; gains ranged from 25 to 50 per cent. On an average, homes in Negro tracts increased in value 61 per cent, those in white tracts 35 per cent, those in integrated neighborhoods 45 per cent, those in changing neighborhoods 42 per cent. Ross says his is the first survey to cover all possible tracts in a large number of cities on the basis of impartial census date, although earlier surveys of isolated census tracts have indicated that home values rise rather than fall during integration. He attributes the marked gain in property values in Negro areas to the rapid rise in extent of the Negro middle class.

Further questions that might come to mind after reading these two articles are:

16. Do statistics tell the whole story?

17. Besides the self-fulfilling prophecy concerning property values mentioned in the article, what other negative self-fulfilling prophecies do people commonly have about Negroes and whites living in the same neighborhood?

18. What is necessary to make a *creative* expectation turn out to be realistic?

19. What other facts can you think of that ought to be investigated in a large scale, concerning integration?

How do you awaken slumbering consciences to take responsibility for developing the human community? It is impossible to awaken consciences and be non-controversial.

In today's social tensions, there are three kinds of mass movement: 1) destructively violent; 2) destructively conservative (persons who defend the status quo and resist all change even when it is necessary); and 3) the mean between these two extremes, which is creatively prophetic.

Honest men honestly disagree over what kinds of conscience-awakening activity are extreme and what kinds are justifiable as necessary. Sometimes a leader or a movement can be right in some ways and wrong in others. It is hard to pronounce absolute judgment upon men and movements.

The following article, written by one of America's most controversial Christian social reformers, explains to some of his critics the kind of soul-searching that goes into any responsible attempt to be a creative prophet.

In reading this article you will be wanting to look for Dr. King's answer to such questions as:

20. Why do men become involved as controversial leaders of protest?

21. What is distinctive about the "non-violent" protest movement?

22. Why is public action, rather than negotiation talks, necessary?

23. When is tension good and when is it bad?

24. How does a person know that "now is the time?"

25. When is civil disobedience justified?

26. Who should be the final judge of Negro progress: whites or Negroes?

Letter from Birmingham City Jail*

My dear Fellow Clergymen,

While confined here in the Birmingham City Jail, I came across your recent statement calling our present activities "unwise and untimely." Seldom, if ever, do I pause to answer criticism of my work and ideas. If I sought to answer all of the criticisms that cross my desk, my secretaries would be engaged in little else in the course of the day and I would have no time for constructive work. But since I feel that you are men of genuine goodwill and your criticisms are sincerely set forth, I would like to answer your statement in what I hope will be patient and reasonable terms.

I think I should give the reason for my being in Birmingham, since you have been influenced by the argument of "outsiders coming in." . . . Several months ago our local affiliate here in Birmingham invited us to be on call to engage in a nonviolent direct action program if such were deemed necessary. We readily consented and when the hour came we lived up to our promises. So I am here, along with several members of my staff, because we were invited here. I am here because I have basic organizational ties here. Beyond this, I am in Birmingham because injustice is here. Just as the eighth century prophets left their little villages and carried their "thus saith the Lord" far beyond the boundaries of their home town, and just as the Apostle Paul left his little village of Tarsus and carried the gospel of Jesus Christ to practically every hamlet and city of the Graeco-Roman world, I too am compelled to carry the gospel of freedom beyond my particular home town. Like Paul, I must constantly respond to the Macedonian call for aid.

Moreover, I am cognizant of the interrelatedness of all communities and states. I cannot sit idly by in Atlanta and not be concerned about what happens in Birmingham. Injustice anywhere is a threat to justice everywhere. We are caught in an inescapable network of mutuality tied in a single garment of des-

---

* By Martin Luther King, Jr.

94

tiny. Whatever affects one directly affects all indirectly. Never again can we afford to live with the narrow, provincial "outside agitator" idea. Anyone who lives inside the United States can never be considered an outsider anywhere in this country.

You deplore the demonstrations that are presently taking place in Birmingham. But I am sorry that your statement did not express a similar concern for the conditions that brought the demonstrations into being. I am sure that each of you would want to go beyond the superficial social analyst who looks merely at effects, and does not grapple with underlying causes. I would not hesitate to say that it is unfortunate that so-called demonstrations are taking place in Birmingham at this time, but I would say in more emphatic terms that it is even more unfortunate that the white power structure of this city left the Negro community with no other alternative.

In any nonviolent campaign there are four basic steps: 1) collection of the facts to determine whether injustices are alive; 2) negotiation; 3) self-purification; and 4) direct action. . . .

You may well ask, "Why direct action? Why sit-ins, marches, etc.? Isn't negotiation a better path?" You are exactly right in your call for negotiation. Indeed, this is the purpose of direct action. Nonviolent direct action seeks to create such a crisis and establish such creative tension that a community that has constantly refused to negotiate is forced to confront the issue. It seeks so to dramatize the issue that it can no longer be ignored. I just referred to the creation of tension as a part of the work of the nonviolent resister. This may sound rather shocking. But I must confess that I am not afraid of the word tension. I have earnestly worked and preached against violent tension, but there is a type of constructive nonviolent tension that is necessary for growth. Just as Socrates felt that it was necessary to create a tension in the mind so that individuals could rise from the bondage of myths and half-truths to the unfettered realm of creative analysis and objective appraisal, we must see the need of having nonviolent gadflies to create the kind of tension in society that will help men rise from the dark depths of prejudice and racism to the majestic heights of understanding and brotherhood. So the purpose of the direct action is to create a situation so crisis-packed that it will inevitably open the door to negotiation. . . .

My friends, I must say to you that we have not made a single gain in civil rights without determined legal and nonviolent pressure. History is the long and tragic story of the fact that privileged groups seldom give up their privileges voluntarily. Individuals may see the moral light and voluntarily give up their unjust posture; but as Reinhold Niebuhr has reminded us, groups are more immoral than individuals.

We know through painful experience that freedom is never voluntarily given by the oppressor; it must be demanded by the oppressed. Frankly I have never yet engaged in a direct action movement that was "well timed," according to the timetable of those who have not suffered unduly from the disease of segregation. For years now I have heard the word "Wait!" It rings in the ear of every Negro with a piercing familiarity. This "wait" has almost always meant "never." It has been a tranquilizing thalidomide, relieving the emotional stress for a moment, only to give birth to an ill-formed infant of frustration. We must come to see with the distinguished jurist of yesterday that "justice too long delayed is justice denied." We have waited for more than three hundred and forty years for our constitutional and God-given rights. The nations of Asia and Africa are moving with jet-like speed toward the goal of political independence and we still creep at horse and buggy pace toward the gaining of a cup of coffee at a lunch counter.

I guess it is easy for those who have never felt the stinging darts of segregation to say wait. But when you have seen vicious mobs lynch your mothers and fathers at will and drown your sisters and brothers at whim; when you have seen hate-filled policemen curse, kick, brutalize, and even kill your black brothers and sisters with impunity; when you see the vast majority of your twenty million Negro brothers smothering in an air-tight cage of poverty in the midst of an affluent society; when you suddenly find your tongue twisted and your speech stammering as you seek to explain to your six-year-old daughter why she can't go to the public amusement park that has just been advertised on television, and see tears welling-up in her little eyes when she is told that Funtown is closed to colored children, and see the depressing clouds of inferiority begin to form in her little mental sky, and see her begin to distort her little personality by unconsciously developing a bitterness toward white people; when you have to concoct an answer for a five-year-old son asking in agonizing pathos: "Daddy, why do white people treat colored people so mean?"; when you take a cross country drive and find it necessary to sleep night after night in the uncomfortable corners of your automobile because no motel will accept you; when you are humiliated day in and day out by nagging signs reading "white" men and "colored"; when your first name becomes "nigger" and your middle name becomes "boy" (however old you are) and your last name becomes "John," and when your wife and mother are never given the respected title "Mrs."; when you are harried by day and haunted by night by the fact that you are a Negro, living constantly at tip-toe stance never quite knowing what to expect next, and plagued with inner fears and outer resentments; when you are forever fighting a degenerating sense of "nobodiness";—then you will understand why we find it difficult to wait. . . .

You express a great deal of anxiety over our willingness to break laws. This is certainly a legitimate concern. Since we so diligently urge people to obey the Supreme Court's decision of 1954 outlawing segregation in the public schools, it is rather strange and paradoxical to find us consciously breaking laws. One may well ask, "How can you advocate breaking some laws and obeying others?" The answer is found in the fact that there are two types of laws: There are *just* laws and there are *unjust* laws. I would be the first to advocate obeying just laws. One has not only a legal but moral responsibility to obey just laws. Conversely, one has a moral responsibility to disobey unjust laws. I would agree with St. Augustine that "An unjust law is no law at all."

Now what is the difference between the two? How does one determine when a law is just or unjust? A just law is a man-made code that squares with the moral law or the law of God. An unjust law is a code that is out of harmony with the moral law. To put it in the terms of Saint Thomas Aquinas, an unjust law is a human law that is not rooted in eternal and natural law. Any law that uplifts human personality is just. Any law that degrades human personality is unjust. All segregation statutes are unjust because segregation distorts the soul and damages the personality. It gives the segregator a false sense of superiority and the segregated a false sense of inferiority. . . .

Let us turn to a more concrete example of just and unjust laws. An unjust law is a code that a majority inflicts on a minority that is not binding on itself. This is *difference* made legal. On the other hand a just law is a code that a majority compels a minority to follow that it is willing to follow itself. This is *sameness* made legal.

Let me give another explanation. An unjust law is a code inflicted upon a minority which that minority had no part in enacting or creating because they did not have the unhampered right to vote. Who can say the legislature of Alabama which set up the segregation laws was democratically elected? Throughout the state of Alabama all types of conniving methods are used to prevent Negroes from becoming registered voters and there are some counties without a single Negro registered to vote despite the fact that the Negro constitutes a majority of the population. Can any law set up in such a state be considered democratically structured? . . .

I hope you can see the distinction I am trying to point out. In no sense do I advocate evading or defying the law as the rabid segregationist would do. This would lead to anarchy. One who breaks an unjust law must do it *openly, lovingly* (not hatefully as the white mothers did in New Orleans when they were seen on television screaming "nigger, nigger, nigger") and with a willingness to accept the penalty. I submit that an individual who breaks a law that conscience tells him is unjust, and willingly accepts the penalty by staying in jail to arouse the conscience of the community over its injustice, is in reality expressing the very highest respect for law.

Of course there is nothing new about this kind of civil disobedience. . . . It was practiced superbly by the early Christians who were willing to face hungry lions and the excruciating pain of chopping blocks, before submitting to certain unjust laws of the Roman Empire. To a degree academic freedom is a reality today because Socrates practiced civil disobedience.

We can never forget that everything Hitler did in Germany was "legal" and everything the Hungarian freedom fighters did in Hungary was "illegal." It was "illegal" to aid and comfort a Jew in Hitler's Germany. But I am sure that, if I had lived in Germany during that time, I would have aided and comforted my Jewish brothers even though it was illegal. If I lived in a communist country today where certain principles dear to the Christian faith are suppressed, I believe I would openly advocate disobeying these anti-religious laws.

I must make two honest confessions to you, my Christian and Jewish brothers. First I must confess that over the last few years I have been gravely disappointed with the white moderate. I have almost reached the regrettable conclusion that the Negroes' great stumbling block in the stride toward freedom is not the

White Citizens' "Counciler" or the Ku Klux Klanner, but the white moderate who is more devoted to "order" than to justice; who prefers a negative peace which is the absence of tension to a positive peace which is the presence of justice; who constantly says "I agree with you in the goal you seek, but I can't agree with your methods of direct action"; who paternalistically feels that he can set the time-table for another man's freedom; who lives by the myth of time and who constantly advised the Negro to wait until a "more convenient season." Shallow understanding from people of good will is more frustrating than absolute misunderstanding from people of ill will. Lukewarm acceptance is much more bewildering than outright rejection. . . .

Actually, we who engage in nonviolent direct action are not the creators of tension. We merely bring to the surface the hidden tension that is already alive. We bring it out in the open where it can be seen and dealt with. Like a boil that can never be cured as long as it is covered up but must be opened with all its pusflowing ugliness to the natural medicines of air and light, injustice must likewise be exposed, with all of the tension its exposing creates, to the light of human conscience and the air of national opinion before it can be cured. . . .

If I have said anything in this letter that is an overstatement of the truth and is indicative of an unreasonable impatience, I beg you to forgive me. If I have said anything in this letter that is an understatement of the truth and is indicative of my having a patience that makes me patient with anything less than brotherhood, I beg God to forgive me. . . .

Yours for the cause of
Peace and Brotherhood

Martin Luther King, Jr.

Discrimination and the Christian conscience*

Fifteen years ago, when this nation was devoting its energies to a World War designed to maintain human freedom, the Catholic Bishops of the United States issued a prayerful warning to their fellow citizens. We called for the extension of full freedom within the confines of our beloved country. Specifically, we noted the problems faced by Negroes in obtaining the rights that are theirs as Americans.

The statement of 1943 said in part:

In the Providence of God there are among us millions of fellow citizens of the Negro race. *We owe to these fellow citizens, who have contributed so largely to the development of our country, and for whose welfare history imposes on us a special obligation of justice,*** to see that they have in fact the rights which are given them in our Constitution. This means not only political equality, but also fair economic and educational opportunities, a just share in public welfare projects, good housing without exploitation, and a full chance for the social advancement of their race.

In the intervening years, considerable progress was made in achieving these goals. The Negro race, brought to this country in slavery, continued its quiet but determined march toward the goal of equal rights and equal opportunity. During and after the

---

* Statement of the Catholic Bishops, 1958.
** Italics are our own emphasis.

100

Second World War, great and even spectacular advances were made in the obtaining of voting rights, good education, better-paying jobs, and adequate housing. Through the efforts of men of good will, of every race and creed and from all parts of the nation, the barriers of prejudice and discrimination were slowly but inevitably eroded.

Because this method of quiet conciliation produced such excellent results, we have preferred the path of action to that of exhortation. Unfortunately, however, it appears that in recent years the issues have become confused and the march toward justice and equality has been slowed, if not halted, in some areas. The transcendent moral issues involved have become obscured, and possibly forgotten.

Our nation now stands divided by the problem of compulsory segregation of the races and the opposing demand for racial justice. No region of our land is immune from strife and division resulting from this problem. In one area, the key issue may concern the schools. In another it may be conflicts over housing. Job discrimination may be the focal point in still other sectors. But all these issues have one main point in common. They reflect the determination of our Negro people, and we hope the overwhelming majority of our white citizens, to see that our colored citizens obtain their full rights as given to them by God, the Creator of all, and guaranteed by the democratic traditions of our nation.

There are many facets to the problems raised by the quest for racial justice. There are issues of law, of history, of economics, and of sociology. There are questions of procedure and technique. There are conflicts in cultures. Volumes have been written on each of these phases. Their importance we do not deny. But the time has come, in our considered and prayerful judgment, to cut through the maze of secondary or less essential issues and to come to the heart of the problem.

The heart of the race question is moral and religious. It concerns the rights of man and our attitude toward our fellow man. If our attitude is governed by the great Christian law of love of neighbor and respect for his rights, then we can work out harmoniously the techniques for making legal, educational, economic, and social adjustments. But if our hearts are poisoned by hatred, or even indifference toward the welfare and rights of our fellow men, then our nation faces a grave internal crisis.

101

No one who bears the name of Christian can deny the universal love of God for all mankind. When Our Lord and Savior, Jesus Christ, "took on the form of man" (Phil. 2, 7) and walked among men, He taught as the first two laws of life the love of God and the love of fellow man. "By this shall all men know that you are my disciples, that you have love, one for the other." (John, 13, 35) He offered His life in sacrifice for all mankind. His parting mandate to His followers was to "teach all nations." (Matt. 28, 19)

Our Christian faith is of its nature universal. It knows not the distinctions of race, color, or nationhood. The missionaries of the Church have spread throughout the world, visiting with equal impartiality nations such as China and India, whose ancient cultures antedate the coming of the Savior, and the primitive tribes of the Americas. The love of Christ, and the love of the Christian, knows no bounds. In the words of Pope Pius XII, addressed to American Negro publishers twelve years ago, "All men are brothers in Jesus Christ; for He, though God, became also man, became a member of the human family, a brother of all." (May 27, 1946)

Even those who do not accept our Christian tradition should at least acknowledge that God has implanted in the souls of all men some knowledge of the natural moral law and a respect for its teachings. Reason alone taught philosophers through the ages respect for the sacred dignity of each human being and the fundamental rights of man. Every man has an equal right to life, to justice before the law, to marry and rear a family under human conditions, and to an equitable opportunity to use the good of this earth for his needs and those of his family.

From these solemn truths, there follow certain conclusions vital for a proper approach to the problems that trouble us today. *First, we must repeat the principle*—embodied in our Declaration of Independence—*that all men are equal in the sight of God.* By equal we mean that they are created by God and redeemed by His Divine Son, that they are bound by His Law, and that God desires them as His friends in the eternity of Heaven. This fact confers upon all men human dignity and human rights .

Men are unequal in talent and achievement. They differ in culture and personal characteristics.

Some are saintly; some seem to be evil; most are men of

102

good will, though beset with human frailty. On the basis of personal differences we may distinguish among our fellow men, remembering always the admonition: "Let him who is without sin . . . cast the first stone . . ." (Jn. 8, 7) But discrimination based on the accidental fact of race or color, and as such injurious to human rights regardless of personal qualities or achievements, cannot be reconciled with the truth that God has created all men with equal rights and equal dignity.

Secondly, we are bound to love our fellow man. The Christian love we bespeak is not a matter of emotional likes or dislikes. *It is a firm purpose to do good to all men, to the extent that ability and opportunity permit.*

Among all races and national groups, class distinctions are inevitably made on the basis of like-mindedness of a community of interests. Such distinctions are normal and constitute a universal social phenomenon. They are accidental, however, and are subject to change as conditions change. It is unreasonable and injurious to the rights of others that a factor such as race, by and of itself, should be made a cause of discrimination and a basis for unequal treatment in our mutual relations.

The question then arises: Can enforced segregation be reconciled with the Christian view of our fellow man? In our judgment it cannot, and this for two fundamental reasons.

1) *Legal segregation, or any form of compulsory segregation, in itself and by its very nature imposes a stigma of inferiority upon the segregated people.* Even if the now obsolete Court doctrine of "separate but equal" had been carried out to the fullest extent, so that all public and semi-public facilities were in fact equal, there is nonetheless the judgment that an entire race, by the sole fact of race and regardless of individual qualities, is not fit to associate on equal terms with members of another race. We cannot reconcile such a judgment with the Christian view of man's nature and rights. Here again it is appropriate to cite the language of Pope Pius XII: "God did not create a human family made up of segregated, dissociated, mutually independent members. No; He would have them all united by the bond of total love of Him and consequent self-dedication to assisting each other to maintain that bond intact." (September 7, 1956)

2) *It is a matter of historical fact that segregation in our country has led to oppressive conditions and the denial of basic*

103

human rights for the Negro. This is evident in the fundamental fields of education, job opportunity, and housing. Flowing from these areas of neglect and discrimination are problems of health and the sordid train of evils so often associated with the consequent slum conditions. Surely Pope Pius XII must have had these conditions in mind when he said just two months ago: "It is only too well known, alas, to what excesses pride of race and racial hate can lead. The Church has always been energetically opposed to attempts of genocide or practices arising from what is called the 'color bar.' " (September 5, 1958)

One of the tragedies of racial oppression is that the evils we have cited are being used as excuses to continue the very conditions that so strongly fostered such evils. Today we are told that Negroes, Indians, and also some Spanish-speaking Americans differ too much in culture and achievements to be assimilated in our schools, factories, and neighborhoods. Some decades back the same charge was made against the immigrant, Irish, Jewish, Italian, Polish, Hungarian, German, Russian. In both instances differences were used by some as a basis for discrimination and even for bigoted ill-treatment. The immigrant, fortunately, has achieved his rightful status in the American community. Economic opportunity was wide open and educational equality was not denied to him.

Negro citizens seek these same opportunities. They wish an education that does not carry with it any stigma of inferiority. They wish economic advancement based on merit and skill. They wish their civil rights as American citizens. They wish acceptance based upon proved ability and achievement. No one who truly loves God's children will deny them this opportunity.

To work for this principle amid passions and misunderstandings will not be easy. It will take courage. But quiet and persevering courage has always been the mark of a true follower of Christ.

We urge that concrete plans in this field be based on prudence. Prudence may be called a virtue that inclines us to view problems in their proper perspective. It aids us to use the proper means to secure our aim.

The problems we inherit today are rooted in decades, even centuries, of custom and cultural patterns. Changes in deep-rooted attitudes are not made overnight. When we are confronted with complex and far-reaching evils, it is not a sign of weakness or timidity to distinguish among remedies and reforms. Some changes are more necessary than others. Some are relatively easy to achieve. Others seem impossible at this time. What may succeed in one area may fail in another.

It is a sign of wisdom, rather than weakness, to study carefully the problems we face, to prepare for advances, and to by-pass the non-essential if it interferes with essential progress. *We may well deplore a gradualism that is merely a cloak for inaction. But we equally deplore rash impetuosity that would sacrifice the achievements of decades in ill-timed and ill-considered ventures.* In concrete matters we distinguish between prudence and inaction by asking the question: Are we sincerely and earnestly acting to solve these problems? We distinguish between prudence and rashness by seeking the prayerful and considered judgment of experienced counselors who have achieved success in meeting similar problems.

For this reason we hope and earnestly pray that responsible and sober-minded Americans of all religious faiths, in all areas of our land, will seize the mantle of leadership from the agitator and the racist. It is vital that we act now and act decisively. All must act quietly, courageously, and prayerfully before it is too late.

For the welfare of our nation we call upon all to root out from their hearts bitterness and hatred. The tasks we face are indeed difficult. But hearts inspired by Christian love will surmount these difficulties.

Clearly, then, these problems are vital and urgent. May God give this nation the grace to meet the challenge it faces. For the sake of generations of future Americans, and indeed of all humanity, we cannot fail.

Signed by members of the Administrative Board, National Catholic Welfare Conference, in the name of the Bishops of the United States November 14, 1958.

Francis Cardinal Spellman, Archbishop of New York
James Francis Cardinal McIntyre, Archbishop of Los Angeles
Francis P. Keough, Archbishop of Baltimore
Karl J. Alter, Archbishop of Cincinnati
Joseph E. Ritter, Archbishop of St. Louis
William O. Brady, Archbishop of St. Paul
Albert G. Meyer, Archbishop of Chicago
Patrick A. O'Boyle, Archbishop of Washington
Leo Binz, Archbishop of Dubuque
Emmet M. Walsh, Bishop of Youngstown
Joseph M. Gilmore, Bishop of Helena
Albert R. Zuroweste, Bishop of Belleville

Outline for Analyzing Socio-Economic Problems

	ECONOMIC	POLITICAL	CULTURAL

FACTORS
  connected
  with the
  problem			

COMMON OPINIONS or PREJUDICES			

FACTS
  and
  how to
  get them			

CHRISTIAN EVALUATION of the facts			
SOLUTIONS			